THE DEMAND PRINCIPLE

Your Invisible Guide

To Easily

Manifest Anything

Peggy McColl

New York Times Best-Selling Author

The Manifestation Mentor

ISBN: 1989756336

Published by:

Hasmark Publishing International

Important Disclaimers

The author has done their best to present accurate and up-to-date information in this book, but cannot guarantee that the information is correct or will suit your particular situation. Further, the publisher has used its best efforts in preparing this book, and the information provided herein is provided "as is."

We can't guarantee any results from the use of our programs or any of the information contained in this book, though we genuinely believe that this information will help you reach your goals. Like with any program, your results are limited by your willingness to take action as well as factors outside of your control and our control. By reading this book and enrolling in any programs you hereby understand the potential risks when embarking upon a goal achievement journey of any kind and are fully aware and take responsibility for your own results holding Peggy McColl and Dynamic Destinies Inc. harmless.

This is intended for informational purposes only and should not be used as the primary basis for an investment decision. Consult a financial advisor for your personal situation. Please consider the investment objectives, risks, fees, and expenses carefully before investing in anything. Past performance does not guarantee future results.

For more disclaimers that may apply, please view the most up to date information on: http://www.peggymccoll.com

Cover design by Trace Haskins
Book layout by Trace Haskins

First Edition, 2020

"DEMAND... absolutely! Demand the very best from yourself. Quit playing around with your potential, with your life. DEMAND the best life has to offer. I DO and I love my life. Get this book and eat every word."

Bob Proctor

Best-Selling Author of "You Were Born Rich"

"Peggy is a thinker, a doer, and an action taker. Life rewards Peggy and it will you too if you follow The Demand Principle!"

Robert Pascuzzi

Best-Selling Author and Prosperity Teacher

Endorsements

"What I love about this book is that by the end of it if you're not getting the message, clearly, you're missing out on something amazing. The message repeats from chapter to chapter, and at first you think 'OK, I think I got it' but you keep reading, and suddenly… a light bulb goes on in your head and that is when you begin to truly internalize it. Only then can you say, I've GOT THIS—I'm ready to do it! It cost nothing to do, and you have everything to gain. Try it!"

L.L. Tremblay

Author of "Seven Roses"

"Peggy McColl has done it again, this time showing us how to manifest anything. Demand is the key and Peggy has managed to put it into words where anyone can understand, and more importantly, apply her lessons. Pick it up right now!"

Phillip B. Goldfine

Film, Television & Broadway Producer

"I have known Peggy McColl for many years. This book is the epitome of who she is. Peggy has always demanded the best of herself, and those that she does business with. She has accomplished so much in her life because of her mindset. In this book she clearly shows you how to demand for more in your life and then how to follow through to achieve it. This is a must read."

Brian Proctor

VP of Business Development, Proctor Gallagher Institute

"One of the key principles of success is that you look to people who have demonstrated by their results that they know what they are doing and then do EXACTLY what they tell you to do. Peggy McColl has demonstrated by her results that she is a master at manifesting, and in this book, she tells you EXACTLY what to do. The principles and she, as a person, changed my life. Allow her to change yours!"

Anders Hansen

Illusionist, Keynote-Performer, Change-Maker

Dedication

I demand this book be dedicated
to my friend Mick.
:-)

Table of Contents

Acknowledgements

There are so many people who have been influential, instrumental and utterly supportive of the work that I do, and it is with enormous gratitude that I acknowledge some of them here.

Family first has always been and always will be my priority. I am blessed with the most amazing family and for this, I am most grateful.

My husband Denis, who is my soulmate and my partner in life. Thank you for the unwavering support you provide to me always in all ways. You are a blessing in my life, and I thank God every day to be your wife.

My son Michel, who has always been and always will be my greatest inspiration. Being your Mom is the greatest gift in my life and I cherish you and love you more than you will ever know.

My grandson James, who is the brightest light, and as I often tell him – he is "the best part of my life." James is the epitome of love, kindness, and generosity. I love your smile and your big heart.

To my daughter-in-law Kayla, who is part of the Dynamic Destinies Inc. team and a valued part of our family too. You are radiant, loving, giving and kind. You always impress me with your common-sense, calm, and gentle approach to everything.

To my stepdaughter Karine, son-in-law Rob, and our precious grandchildren Noah and Lila, you are all a gift of love and joy. Marrying Denis has brought this incredible blessing of my extended family and for this, I am grateful.

To my sister Judy, who owns and runs Hasmark Publishing who kindly published this book, as well as many others and is a constant support for everything I am doing to serve people in positive ways.

My team at Dynamic Destinies Inc. is an extraordinary group of individuals who are all committed to bringing more value to the world in only positive ways. For all of you, Trace, Sabrina, Selin, Eric and Kayla, I am grateful. Thank you for all you do.

Trace Haskins deserves an extra shout-out here as he inserted extra love and attention on this book that made it even more valuable. You constantly surprise me with your giving nature, authenticity and your exceptional talent. Feel so blessed to co-serve with you.

To my mentor and friend Bob Proctor for being the guide who lead me on the path to a magical life.

To my friend Brian Proctor who is always there for me as a valued friend. It gives me great comfort knowing that I can always count on you. Your example of leaving people with the impression of increase inspires me to give more.

To Jayne Lowell, who started as a client and quickly became a friend. Our friendship is one of the greatest gifts in my life. We may not be related by birth, but you are definitely my soul-sister.

To Phil Goldfine, my friend and co-creator of many programs, I love and appreciate how you always inspire me to be more, do more and serve more. You are a wonderful example of the principles shared in this book and an inspiration to me and so many others.

And, finally to my cherished friend Mick – to whom this book is dedicated – thank you for putting your heart and soul into helping me create this book. You did the heavy-lifting and I am so grateful for you. A big thank you for being a constant source of joy, love and a ton of fun in my life. You are loved and appreciated.

Preface

The Keys to YOUR Kingdom

The Demand Principle has been a long time coming. This message is a bit different from any of the other books and/or materials you may find. However, do not underestimate the enormous power and potential of applying what you are about to discover.

Herein lies a secret... a *powerful*, *important*, *life-changing* and *simple* methodology that has the potential to change your life in every way... when you follow it. You may have studied personal development before, or this may be your first introduction, but I will tell you this ... what you are about to learn in this book has completely changed my life and other people's lives in magical and glorious ways – and it can change yours, too.

But reading this book isn't enough — you must create *demands* if you want to change your future.

Introduction

In 1989, I was working at a Word Processor Manufacturing Company in Toronto, Ontario, Canada and one day my employer announced that every employee would be required to attend a mandatory personal development seminar the following week. I thought it was a ridiculous waste of my valuable time, and despite my best efforts, I couldn't wriggle out of it.

The day of the seminar arrived and showing up late was the only option I found in order to protest having to attend. Standing at the back of the packed auditorium, I found every seat taken. From the stage, the Master of Ceremonies caught my eye. *"Young lady – there's an open seat up here,"* she said, waving. Every head in the place spun around to gawk at me. Red-faced, I dragged myself to the front and slumped into my seat, secretly pledging to myself not to listen to anything the speaker, Bob Proctor, had to say.

In those days, I had the worst attitude of anyone I knew, but I didn't understand how destructive a bad attitude was and I didn't realize at the time that I had one. Almost instantly, the speaker's message had somehow penetrated my invisible protective shield, and I soon found myself mesmerized by his every word. It seemed as though he was talking directly to me and from time to time, he looked me squarely in the eyes.

I was inspired when he quoted Vernon Howard and said, *"You can't escape a prison if you don't know you're in one."* All at once, moments from my life flashed before my eyes. All of the bad feelings I had ever felt came rushing back: the shame for growing up in such a shabby little house, the embarrassment for having to wear hand-me-down tattered clothes to school, the humiliation I endured for receiving low marks on my report cards. I realized that in every circumstance I had always blamed someone else for my results instead of taking responsibility for them myself.

Right there in the front row of the auditorium, I was in the midst of my first real "attitude adjustment" and, at that point, I truly had no idea how much my life was going to positively change.

Without judgment or defensiveness, I looked at how I had been showing up in life — MY LIFE — and I wasn't satisfied. I wanted more… something different… significant… better for myself. For the first time, I became aware that I had the power to change my life and the direction of my future.

At the time, I couldn't have known how that single event would change the course of my life any more than you can know the potential this book has in changing yours. In the following chapters, I will reveal to you the most powerful secrets to success that I have discovered since reluctantly attending my first personal development seminar.

Right now, you have everything you need to live the life of your dreams.

(Note to the reader: The previous line is one worthwhile highlighting.)

Over the years, I have developed an extremely effective and easy strategy that I now follow every day of my life. And if you follow it, you too will gain the power to reset the course of your life and change your results forever.

Soon, you'll look back at where you are now and wonder where your new life was hiding all this time. Previously, the only thing that had been missing was the Demand Principle. So…

Are you ready to change your destiny and create the life of your dreams?

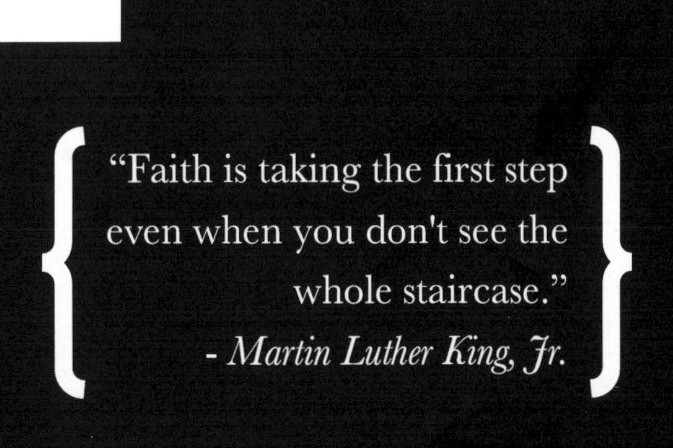

PART ONE

CONCEIVE

Chapter One

The Meaning of Demand

You can have, do, or be anything you want within the laws of nature. Hearing that may seem outrageous, but it's true. Many of the accomplished people in the world have applied what you are about to discover. They created extraordinary results and live completely fulfilling, abundant and rewarding lives. You can do it too!

All you have to do is know what you want and, *demand* it in a certain way, and demand more of yourself.

"Isn't it offensive, bold, or even rude, to demand something?" you may ask. Many people recoil at the very thought of demanding what they want out of life.

A reaction like this only occurs because you may not understand what the meaning of *demand* is in the context that I prescribe. Let me explain.

According to the dictionary, the definition is:

de · mand: /dəˈmand/, *(noun)* -
an insistent and peremptory request made as if by right.

DEMAND is such a misunderstood word. It is a *request* in which you ask for what you want, *knowing* the outcome you desire *will happen without question or further discussion*… **As if it is already done.** There's nothing outrageous about that.

So, at this point, you may be asking, *"how can I use the Demand Principle to make my desire real?"* The answer is simple …demand it! But like everything, there is a process you must follow.

Everything starts from a desire. But a desire is merely an idea unless and until it is accepted and acted upon. I once read that ideas are like slippery fish — if you don't gaff them immediately, they'll get away. Outlined below is the process that a desire must go through to harden into a demand.

The 4 Steps:

Desire

Decide

Dedicate

Demand

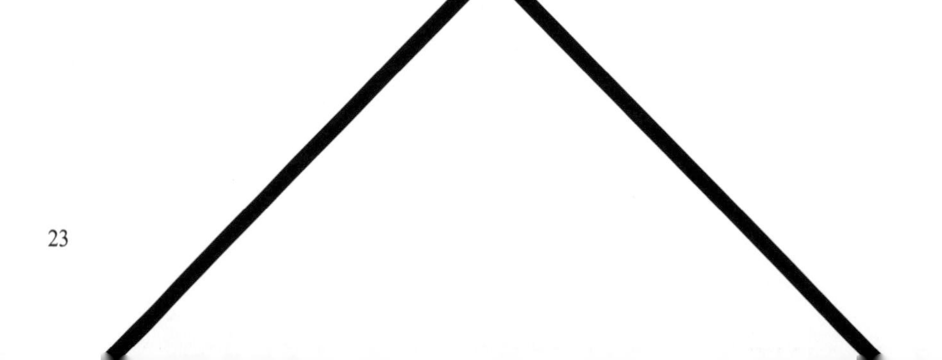

Step One: **Desire**

Desires are the things you yearn for; have a longing to experience. Inside you feel an intense burning desire. Be open to your desires. Pay attention to what inspires you. If you have the desire, you have the ability to achieve it.

You might be surprised to learn that the first step, to determine your desires, is so easy, although many people don't move past this step in the process because they are immediately trying to figure out the "how". You must know this – you do NOT have to know how you will bring your desire into your reality when you decide it's what you want. To immediately know how is like "putting the cart before the horse". The belief that you must know how to manifest something the moment you desire it is a false belief! Do not allow your present results, or disempowering beliefs, to hold you back.

When a desire reveals itself to you in the form of a thought or a feeling, it is coming from an infinite source; the Universe. Occasionally, an idea so powerful shows up that it catches you off guard and grabs your attention. It may even be regarded as ludicrous, either by yourself or others. When this happens, your only job is to recognize it and ask yourself, *"Do I want it?"* If the answer is a resounding "yes" (even though you will have no idea how you are going to accomplish this desire), you are already ready to move onto the next step. The best way to move this desire into form, is to go to the next step … to decide.

Step Two: **Decide**

The second step in the process is to make an irrevocable decision to commit to your desire. People are often reluctant about making decisions, mostly because many of us weren't ever taught how to properly make decisions, or even the importance of making decisions. However, if you want to convert your desire into something more, you must decide to go for it.

So how do you decide? Simply ask yourself, "*Do I really want it?*" The step of making a decision represents the next right action required for you to convert your desire into a demand. When you decide, remember to make the decision based upon how you feel and ignore any "logic" or "good excuses" as to why you cannot or should not proceed. If you toss any negatives aside, and you feel positively about your desire, that's your indicator that "YES" is the right decision.

This "decision" step is one of the most important steps you can take in this process, as well as in your life. Anything magnificent that has ever been created or achieved in the world by anyone came as a result of one thing: the decision to make it happen.

Step Three: **Dedicate**

The third step in the process requires dedication. I like to think of it like this: Once you've decided that the desire is worthy of your attention, you plant it into your consciousness, like you would plant a seed into the fertile garden of your mind. Once it's planted, you nurture it, care for it, feed and water it by being dedicated to it. By being dedicated, you are nourishing it and giving it positive energy. You dedicate yourself to it for as long as is necessary for it to bloom.

With our seeds of desire, the component of time is not known; we do not know how long it will take for our desire to manifest. We must be unconcerned with time and feel and imagine that our seed is already fully grown right now in the present moment. When we nourish it in this fashion, we are fully dedicated and committed to our desired outcome, and it is therefore alive – and thriving – whether beneath the surface of what we can see, or out amongst the glorious sunlight!

Step Four: **Demand**

The fourth step in the process is to place your demand. Up until now, you've created a desire ... decided to go for it ... agreed to dedicate yourself to its manifestation ... and now, you demand yourself – in concert with the powers of the Universe – to manifest it. When you make this demand, you're declaring your own destiny; and you are believing 100% in it, knowing that by completing this process, fate is sealed and it is done.

Demand Dismisses All Doubt

Have you ever wondered why some people spend so much time, effort and energy on an idea only to give up on it when the first obstacle presents itself? It's as if they've hit a home run and suddenly run out of gas rounding third base.

What happens is, people often allow their external circumstances and conditions to dictate how they act and feel instead of understanding the last step in the process to the realization of their dream (to demand).

Everything human-made started from a desire — it was once something intangible, something invisible in someone's mind until they demanded it to harden into reality. Here, the name of the game is commitment.

No desire, no decision, no thought and no demand (also known as a "goal") could ever come to fruition without the one who conjured the desire *committing* to its attainment.

You must be so "jazzed", so "pumped", so thoroughly "enthused" about your idea – essentially "head over heels in love" with your desire, constantly feeding it your thought energy as well as taking action on it – that you know without even a sprinkle of doubt that its attainment is certain.

You must know with a high level of certainty that no matter what your demand is, it is already yours, and the secret key is to FEEL as if it is here now; by demanding it, you've instantly called it into existence.

Here's an example of how it works. Imagine that you're sitting in a restaurant and the server comes to your table. You place your order, then you sit back and wait expectantly for your food to arrive. As you wait expectantly, you don't wring your hands and anxiously wonder if the server will bring your food... And, you don't run into the kitchen to harass the kitchen staff about whether or not they will fulfill your order. Instead, you wait patiently at the table engaged in a nice conversation with friends until your food comes, because you **know with certainty** that your order will soon arrive.

When making a demand, there can be no room for denial, refusal or doubt. You must **know with certainty** that it is already accomplished. Remember the definition of the word demand as shared previously?

de · mand: /dəˈmand/, *(noun)* -
an insistent and peremptory request made as if by right.

The fact that you were capable of dreaming up the idea of your demand — that you could summon it into existence by means of your imagination — dictates that it must be met. You cannot dream up something that you cannot accomplish.

It is important for you to know that this process works on anything; from manifesting a dream home to manifesting perfect health, manifesting a soulmate, manifesting abundance and anything else that you desire.

Pets give an excellent illustration of how the Demand Principle works. When dogs want something—food, water, to be taken for a walk, a scratch behind the ear — they express their demands upon us with insistence. They expect to be fed, to be given water, to go for a walk, to get a scratch behind their ear. They assume their demand will be met.

Is their demand done in a confrontational, aggressive, or braggadocios way? No, they do it differently…with confidence, love, and expectation. They insist on their demands and make demands as if they were their right.

Animals have an understanding that their demands will be fulfilled—they KNOW it. On the other hand, oftentimes when a person makes a demand and it doesn't materialize right away, they give up on it, let it go and succumb to the idea that it must not have been meant to be. Fortunately, through understanding the Demand Principle, it doesn't have to be that way.

As babies, we naturally understood the Demand Principle, but as we grew into adults -- through the conditioning of those who raised us as well as the rest of society -- we forgot all about it. Robert A. Russell wrote, *"[As a child] You not only accepted but demanded in a loud imperious voice the things that gave you emotional and physical comfort."*

The first time I heard about making demands, and before I fully understood how it worked, it made me curious. To me, how anyone could find it appealing was surprising. It seemed bold, egotistical and entitled—that is, until I read a story about two salesmen who made a sales call to a local business.

The two salesmen entered the business owner's office, shook hands, then took a seat. Behind the owner's desk, on the back wall hung a sign that read: *"I demand $250,000"*.

The meeting started and ended with neither salesmen mentioning the sign.

Several months passed, and they returned to business and found themselves in the owner's office again. This time, the sign on the back wall read: *"I demand $1,000,000"*.

The jump from $250,000 to $1,000,000 got their attention. One of them finally mustered the courage to ask,

"Last time we were here, your sign said, 'I demand $250,000,' now it says, 'I demand $1,000,000.' What's with these signs?"

The businessman chuckled, leaning in as if to share a secret. *"Many years ago, someone taught me about how the Demand Principle works. That night, I went home and fashioned a sign demanding $100,000 from the universe. Although it felt odd to me, I remembered being told that it was imperative that I maintain a feeling of confidence, 100% confidence, that $100,000 would show up in my life. And it eventually did. I thought, 'Wow! if it works for $100,000 then it will surely work for more, so I created a new sign: 'I demand $250,000'. And it, too, eventually showed up. Now, I am demanding $1,000,000. I've come to understand that this same methodology will manifest any amount of money that I want, requiring the same level of energy to do it."*

That night, the two salesmen went home and made signs of their own. Both of them eventually received their demands as well.

As soon as I heard this explanation of the Demand Principle, a lightbulb sprang to life in my mind, and it all suddenly made sense. That evening I created a sign of my own. I fixated on a sum of money that would double my personal income, which excited me even though I had no idea how I was going to do it.

Several times a day, I played a game with myself, imagining what I was going to do with the money. I could really see and feel it. I visualized the money already in my bank account. The more I looked at the sign and the more I engaged all my senses in the game, the more I believed my income demand would come to pass. In fact, the more I engaged in these exercises with the imagination, the more it felt like it had already happened.

Religiously practicing this technique, and focusing only on the outcome that I desired… it showed up!

When you make a demand of the universe, you don't have to know how you're going to do it or how much time it'll take to do it, you only need to know it will happen AND connect to the feeling state as if the demand has already materialized in your life. Use your imagination and let it create your world – first inside your mind, then on the outside.

There is no limit to what you can demand (within the laws of nature). The same level of energy to manifest $100,000 can manifest $250,000, or $1,000,000. This is confirmed by Napoleon Hill in his book *Think And Grow Rich* when he declared, *"No more effort is required to aim high in life,* ***to demand abundance and prosperity****, than is required to accept misery and poverty."*

The length of time for a demand to manifest cannot be predicted. The truth is, it'll take as long as it needs to. Your job is to act as if your demand has already arrived and trust in the process.

Exercise:

Begin to think of your desires. What would you love? What would you love to do, be, experience, have, enjoy, achieve, accomplish, earn? Rekindle old ambitions. Revisit lost pursuits. Reignite old flames. Create new flames of desire. You are the creator, the architect of your life.

In daydreams and when your thoughts aren't preoccupied with the menial trivia of life, be quiet and let your mind wander. In fact, let your ideas soar. Revive the long-forgotten dreams of your childhood. Do you remember those farfetched notions you may have had? Breathe life back into them by merely thinking about them again. Be unrealistic and pretend those wild imaginings could come to pass. Your assignment is to simply imagine what you would really love.

If you could have anything and everything you desired...

How would you love to be living?

Who would you become?

Where would you live?

What type of home would you own?

What is your relationship(s) like?

What hobbies would you have?

What income would you love to earn?

Where would you work?

What job would you have?

How would you give?

How or where would you travel?

What vehicles would you own?

How would you contribute?

"Whatever the mind of man
can conceive and believe,
it can achieve."
- *Napoleon Hill*

Chapter Two

Anatomy Of A Good Demand

We've all seen it before: A little boy who throws a temper tantrum at the grocery store because he didn't get any candy. The unhappy CEO who grumbles at himself and his employees in frustration because his company didn't hit its annual target. The teenage girl who sniffles sadly because she didn't make the cheerleading squad. Why didn't these people get what they wanted, and why are so many people unhappy with their results?

Maybe they had unrealistic expectations, or maybe they didn't try hard enough to achieve their desires. I am here to tell you that neither is the case. Most of the time, we rely on less effective "old" ways of doing things instead of examining them from new angles. It's time to take a different approach. It's time to make **definite demands**.

Can you have a thought for a desire, become dedicated to it, decide this is your demand and demand it into existence? Absolutely! You have been given the power to bring the unseen to the seen, as long as you follow a few basic rules.

Your demands must be:

- Inspired by your desires
- Focused
- Clear and definite
- Positive for you
- Positive for others
- Reasonable, in the nature of things; not beyond the realm of possibility
- Felt with emotions
- Present tense (felt as if it is here now)

If the above criteria are followed, your demand will, in time, become your reality. The length of time for it to manifest is simply a guess. The truth is, the time it takes for most demands to manifest into form, is merely a guess. Your responsibility, if you would love to have your demand manifested, is to act and feel as if it has already arrived.

You must know with absolute confidence that your demand will show up and yet feel as if it is here NOW. The fact that you were capable of dreaming it up should serve as the first evidence that it can manifest into reality. That you could summon it into existence by means of your imagination dictates that it will come to pass.

Notice the word "will"? This isn't a "maybe" scenario. Truly, if you follow the guidelines, you can and will manifest every desire you have into reality.

It would be wise to believe that demanding something is your birthright! This has staggering implications in regard to your ability to create a better life for yourself. You need to begin the process by demanding it.

Of course, you will be required to take action for it to come to fruition ... the Law of Attraction is highly misunderstood to work without any action other than visualization, which is not true ... but before you can act, first you must know what it is you want.

For now, just know that you have the ability right where you are, **right now,** to take your first step toward bringing forth whatever it is your heart desires.

Let's say you have a desire to own a new and magnificent waterfront home. You can begin to build a picture of it in your mind using your imagination. What attributes would you love in your new home? How many bedrooms does it have? How many bathrooms? Does it have a garage? Do you have a pool? Which direction are you facing? Do you see the sunset or sunrise? What is your new neighborhood like?

Asking yourself questions like these will help you to define your desires, and visualizing what you want will aid you in refining your picture. You must become the architect, imbuing your vision with as much detail as you possibly can to make it real for you. These are the basic, mechanical parts of your demand.

Now it's time to crank up your imagination's engine by adding feeling and experiences to your visualization. In your mind, start living in your new home. See yourself waking up in the morning in your new home. Make yourself a cup of coffee and smell the aroma in your new kitchen. Imagine doing the dishes in your new sink and feel the water's warmth on your hands as you look at the window and catch the glimpse of a sailboat sailing by. Celebrate your child's birthday, on your sandy beach, and hear your friends and family singing the Happy Birthday song and smell the Sulphur from the blown-out candles. See your dog running around the yard having a blast playing fetch. Imagine all the wonderful experiences you'd love to experience and feel the elation of having them in your new home. See the holiday celebrations you are enjoying with your loved ones. Create vividly real images in your mind that you can become emotionally involved with.

Once you have the mental picture infused with emotion solidly in your being, then it's time to take action on the idea.

A number of years ago, my husband and I decided we wanted to move to a different location, so we started imagining our next dream home. Together, we invested quality time imagining everything we'd love in our next dream home, and it was a wonderful experience. With clear demands, we wrote out a list of the qualities that we were looking for. We searched the internet and visited open houses, but none of the homes on the market matched the picture we had in our minds exactly.

Nonetheless, I stayed connected to the feeling that we had already found our home, purchased it and we were loving living in our new beautiful home located in the perfect area.

It wasn't until one crisp fall day while touring a home at an open house that I walked in the front door and I knew I had found our next home. This home had been listed for sale online. I saw the listing online, but didn't really give it a second thought because the purchase price was more than twice the price of our previous home. Since the owner was hosting an Open House, I decided to check it out.

The moment I walked in the front door I experienced an overwhelmingly wonderful feeling of excitement. This feeling was the same feeling that I had felt while building the picture of us living in our dream home during my visualization practice. All of the wonderful emotions came rushing back.

By following the Demand Principle, we purchased that home even though we had no idea how we were going to pay for it. The asking price of this home was significantly higher than the home we previously owned. Following the guidelines in this book, we not only bought that home, but we are happily residing in this home at the time of the writing of this book.

Quality time spent in the activity of visualizing to figure out where you'd love to live and what kind of home you'd love to live in and the experiences you'd love to experience in your new home will actually speed up the process of making it a reality. Besides, it is a fun and powerful game to play.

You can do this for a dream home; you can do this for anything you desire. ***Anything.***

> "When you make a demand of the universe, you don't have to know how you're going to do it or how much time it'll take to do it, you only need to know that it will happen. Keep the faith!"
>
> \- *Peggy McColl*

Exercise:

Refer to the list you crafted in the previous chapter. Continue to play with your ideas.

Evaluate each demand you wrote down by making sure every one of them meets all criteria outlined in the list above. Invest the time to do this exercise as it is an important part of the process. And, don't put it off – do it right now. You'll thank me later.

{ "A goal properly set
is halfway reached."
– *Zig Ziglar* }

Chapter Three

What Would You Love?

You have the opportunity to use the power of your thought to create positively and on purpose. This is one of the reasons why I love the Demand Principle. Anyone, regardless of past results, can truly change their life for the better and demand it into reality.

Your mind is a powerful tool… powerful beyond measure. Some say it's the most powerful force in the universe. Because of this, you have the ability to use this force, something you were endowed with at birth, to create whatever you can dream up by properly directing well-conceived and laser-focused thoughts.

Put your imagination to work and create images of what you want and completely steer clear of dwelling on what you don't want. If done correctly and consistently, the good you desire will be attracted to you.

Decide what you want.

Let's play a game. Imagine slipping behind the steering wheel of the car of your dreams or exchanging marriage vows with your soulmate or unlocking the door to your dream house and walking in knowing that you just purchased and paid for your dream home with cash. All of these ideas are possible for you if you get your thinking right.

Look around at all the people who live abundant, wealthy and purpose-filled lives — the lifestyle you'd love to live — and, understand, they're no different from you.

Repeat aloud: *"I deserve to live the life of my dreams."* The reality is, you do deserve to live the life of your dreams – and so does the next person.

You've got to play full out and expect good things to come your way with an unwavering knowledge that whatever you want is already yours. Make a committed decision right here, right now that this is going to be your new way of being. You have nothing to lose and everything to gain.

At this point, I think it is important to note that there are different types of demands in many areas of your life that are available to you – and in becoming aware of the different types, you can optimally define your demands. Breaking this down into categories may help you to discover your own desires.

Here are some examples of the different types of demands:

- **Study**: I demand that I commit an hour every day to study positive growth materials.
- **Home**: I demand that I own outright my beautiful home (insert address here – if you have already found the exact home you would love to own) and you are now living in and loving your new home.
- **Behavior:** I demand myself to be only loving, understanding and kind and leave every person I come into contact with the impression of increase.
- **Habit:** I demand that I am in the habit of writing out my highest priority demand every morning and every night, and I demand that I exercise 5 days per week every week.
- **Romance**: I demand that I open myself up to allow my soulmate to come into my life and we are living happily ever after.
- **Professional**: I demand that I attract another XXXX clients and I am serving more people and adding more value to my clientele.
- **Monetary**: I demand that I am easily earning $1,000,000 each and every month in personal income while having fun.

- **Health and well-being**: I demand perfect health and that I am respecting my physical body by nurturing myself with eating healthy food, exercising daily, drinking only healthy beverages and getting a restful sleep every single night, waking up refreshed and ready to take action toward my demands.

- **Spiritual:** I demand that every morning I write in my gratitude journal and genuinely feel grateful for the many gifts in my life.

- **Material Possessions**: I demand that I purchase, own and enjoy driving my brand new fully loaded vehicle that I paid for with cash.

- **Relationship**: I demand that I have only harmonious relationships in my life and these relationships are based on mutual respect, love, appreciation and honor.

The above examples are designed to move you into action to think about the many areas of your life where you can create demands; they are only examples, and your demands can be much more detailed. The most important demand is on you. ***You*** must be the one who demands more of yourself to achieve your goal. This is ***your life*** and if you want to enjoy it, you've got to do this yourself.

Napoleon Hill's Demand

When Napoleon Hill completed his book, he knew the publisher wanted him to come up with a winning title that would send copies of his book flying off the shelves. Every day, he wrote out every title that came to his mind, and every day, the publisher called to hear the latest additions to his list.

None of the more than 500 titles that Napoleon had listed were "right".

One day, the publisher called to say that he needed the title by the following day, or the book would be called, *"Use Your Noodle and Get The Boodle."*

"No!..." Napoleon responded, *"You will ruin me if you use that title!"* The publisher stood firm, telling him he had until the next day to come up with the perfect title.

That night, Napoleon was feeling anxious. He wanted the perfect name for his book, and he needed it in a hurry. His demand started small with quiet, unspecific incantations directed at his subconscious mind as he paced his bedroom floor. As he added more emotion, he started yelling at his subconscious mind to cough up a perfect title.

"You and I have gone a long way together. You've done a lot of things for me—and some things to me. But I've got to have a million-dollar title, and I've got to have it tonight! Do you understand me?"

His ranting grew to such a noise that his upstairs neighbor started banging a broom handle against Napoleon's ceiling telling him to quiet down.

Shortly thereafter, Napoleon, having been satisfied that he'd infused sufficient emotion into his demand that his subconscious mind had received the message, went to bed. Around two o'clock in the morning, the author shot bolt upright and jumped out of bed to write down the title that his subconscious mind had delivered, right on time.

Quickly, he phoned the publisher, who answered in a sleepy voice, *"You've got some nerve calling me in the middle of the night."*

"I've got it!" Napoleon Hill enthusiastically shouted through the phone. *"The million-dollar 'title is 'Think And Grow Rich!'"* The Publisher loved the new title and they released his book that went on to sell several million copies.

Remember, we live in an abundant universe and everything is available to you — in the same way it was available to Napoleon Hill — if you're willing to demand it.

Demand is not about fighting against the grain, nor is it about force. Force negates.

Demand is about perfect, natural, even super-natural alignment with your desire, every moment of every day.

Several years ago, a Publisher contacted me to request that I write a book as part of a book series. When the Publisher asked me to write this book, they did not request a date for when the manuscript would be required to be submitted. (A deadline, or a due date, typically moves people into action).

Without a due date or deadline, I wasn't motivated to write the book. One day late in October I received a call from the Publisher asking me if I could submit the edited manuscript by the 15th of November. I was in the middle of a business trip and wouldn't be returning home for several days. Upon arriving at home, early in November, I dedicated the weekend to write the book. I demanded of myself to write this book in a weekend.

At the time of the demand, I was not sure if I could write a book in a weekend; I had never done that before. However, I accepted the challenge and, as the demand principle dictates, I assumed it was already done and felt the gratitude of this book being completed.

As the weekend approached, my husband told me that his two aunts and their husbands would be joining us for the weekend. They would be arriving on Saturday afternoon and depart on Sunday. Since my husband isn't the cook in the house, I raced out and bought the groceries and planned the meals for our guests. On the Saturday morning I dedicated a few hours to creating the outline for the book. On Sunday morning I woke up at 3am. I felt rested and decided to jump out of bed and head into my office.

I made another demand of myself. I demanded that I write a chapter an hour until the book was completed. By 9pm that evening the book was written and handed over to the editor.

The book was due on the 15th of November, however, on the 13th of November I submitted a fully edited manuscript to the Publisher two days early.

Here's an important point to reflect on with regard to demands:

When you make demands of yourself,
the benefit isn't what you'll get;
the benefit is who you become in the process.

Exercise:

Write out the following question on a notecard and ask yourself:

"What are my demands for all areas of my life?"

Unleash the power of your imagination and pretend whatever it is that you most desire is yours. Jot down ideas as they come to you. You are simply playing in the workshop of your imagination. It is your workshop, and you can create anything and any experience you desire.

"When you discover your mission,
you will feel its demand.
It will fill you with enthusiasm
and a burning desire to get to work on it."
- *W. Clement Stone*

Chapter Four

Suspend Disbelief

Is it truly possible to start with an idea, follow this Demand Principle process, and manifest it into existence?

From over forty years of studying personal development, from applying what you are learning in this book and from personal experience, I can answer with an unequivocal YES!

We've been given a power to bring the unseen into reality by using the powerful tools each of us was born with — OUR MINDS AND OUR EMOTIONS. Often, we have allowed our minds and our emotions to create scenarios in our life that don't feel very good. It is time to demand of yourself to put that kind of behavior in the past, and demand that you remain conscious of your mind and emotional activity – controlling it like your very own Demand Principle Director.

Is it wise to believe that you're entitled to have whatever it is you want? Yes! It is yours by birthright; you need only to realize this truth. And since this is true, it has staggering implications in regard to your ability to create a better life for yourself. You need only demand it.

Of course, action will be required for its attainment, but for now, just know that all you have to do, at this time, is to follow these steps.

Whatever you can see in your mind
and feel in your heart,
you can hold in your hand.

The infamous Dutch painter Vincent van Gogh once said, *"First, I dream my painting, then I paint my dream."* For centuries, philosophers have spoken about the imagination, and visionaries have had their visions, but it has always been the doers who have combined these elements with action to bring their creations to life.

Just think, somebody had a dream to connect everyone on the planet via the Internet; and today, we can scarcely imagine life without it. Somewhere, sometime, someone activated their mind and dreamed it up and it became a reality only by taking action.

This goes for any sort of human advancement for as long as humans have been on earth. It doesn't matter if Vincent Van Gogh's initial vision was the final version of Starry Night or not. What matters is that he first conjured an image, then took action by painting.

It doesn't matter if George Lucas dreamed up the movies we now know as Star Wars or not. What matters is that he took action and moved forward and created them.

It doesn't matter if J.K. Rowling knew – in her imagination – every detail about each of the books in the Harry Potter series or not. What matters is that she took action and wrote them.

Accomplishing your dream requires you dream it, then follow the Demand Principle and take action on your dream.

What stops most people from going after their dreams is themselves. People literally get in their own way. They might say, *"I'd love to do that, but I can't. Maybe someone else can, but I never could."* They give up before they start.

Those who actually go beyond this stage may begin to conjure an image in their minds about how wonderful it would be to realize their dreams while simultaneously and almost in the same breath, say, *"But, I don't know how."* Then, that demeaning little voice inside their head (also known as a "paradigm") goes to work, saying things like: *"You can't do that"* or *"Who do you think you are?"* or *"You? You don't deserve that"* or *"You're not good enough"*.

Listening to these self-sabotaging paradigms and giving in to these self-limiting beliefs will squash your dream every time, unless and until you start believing in the possibility that you can achieve the things you set out to achieve. Then, when these paradigms rear their ugly heads, your belief can politely toss them aside. You **demand** more. You **deserve** better.

So, grab a brush and start painting your dream!

Then see your dream as if it is already here — right here right now.

There was a time when my business was growing at a rapid rate, and I decided to expand my team. I set the intention to continue to grow the business and I sat down and made a list of exactly what I wanted in the team-member we would add. I immediately began affirming it to myself that this was done (feeling as if we already had the perfect new team member on our team). I even recorded the success of the expansion of my team in my Power Life Script® and listened to it over and over (more on the Power Life Script® later).

One night, I was lying in bed, floating in that place between wake and sleep, imagining how wonderful my business' success felt when an idea popped into my mind. *"Ask Judy."*

My sister Judy owned her own business and was very busy, and yet I thought, she would be the perfect person to join my team. The next morning, I woke up, remembering the idea from the night before. Because I have been using the Demand Principle for a long time, I understood that when an idea pops into my head, I need to act on it right then and there... So that same day, I was on the phone with my sister. I told her about my company's growth and how I was looking to expand my team.

"By chance, would you be interested in joining my team on a part-time basis?" I asked, knowing full well that she was already running her own business.

She thought about it for a minute and responded, *"Of course I would,"* and then added on, *"but I'm expensive"* with a chuckle.

We laughed, then I hired her at the rate she wanted. At first, I couldn't believe she had agreed, but, upon further analysis, I realized how important it had been for me to hire a reliable person with a good work ethic, high standards and the trustworthiness on which I could depend to always complete the job on time. Instinctively, I had demanded the ideal person to help me take my business to another level, and I got her.

Focus positive thoughts on the outcome of your demand as if it is already done.

Understand invisible forces are at your service.

Exercise:

Begin paying attention to your inner dialogue also known as self-talk. What is your paradigm saying to you?

When you hear something that doesn't support your demands, makes you feel "less than" or no longer serves you, shift your thinking to something positive.

Write down new beliefs that express the exact opposite of that negative talk.

Speak these affirmations, with emotion, aloud multiple times each day.

“Let us train our minds to desire what the situation demands.”

- *Seneca*

Chapter Five

Give Yourself Permission To Dream Big

Wanting a certain outcome is one thing, but approaching it effectively is another thing altogether. It's time you looked at your demands with a little bit more imagination.

Don't get stuck in the place of what you think you could do. Instead, go for what you would really love, regardless of how big it may be. By recognizing all the resources available to you, you can attract the best possible results you desire.

Your mind is the most powerful resource you have, so use it!

It is time to put on your thinking cap, because your mind is mighty beyond comprehension. It is also untapped and under-utilized.

Most people take their minds for granted! It came to you freely at birth as standard operating equipment, and it is something most people undervalue. However, your mind is, in fact, the most important tool you have at your disposal.

An Interior Designer once came to decorate a spectacular new dream home my husband and I had just bought. *"In preparation for this meeting, I researched you,"* she said excitedly. *"Would you mind sharing some of your life strategies with me? ... because I'm not satisfied with how things are going in my business."* She went on to explain that she was dissatisfied with her income.

"How do you currently earn money?" I asked. As an entrepreneur, a small business owner, and a decorator, she had already shared her hourly rates with me, and they weren't exorbitant, so I was curious to see where her head was in regard to money.

"I earn my income by working with clients, one-on-one, like I'm doing with you," she said.

"How much money did you earn last year?"

"About $40,000."

"Would you like to earn more next year?"

She nodded yes.

"How about $200,000?" It was a number that I had pulled out of thin air, but her reaction to the suggestion surprised me. Her face turned a new shade of red and she seemed to be stunned by the question. The wheels of fear, doubt and worry began turning in her mind, and it became obvious to me that this idea made her very uncomfortable.

"I could never earn that kind of money!" she said defensively. *"That would mean that I'd have to be in front clients 24/7—it's just impossible."*

I smiled warmly and made a suggestion. *"Just entertain the idea of earning the money, not the way you would earn it ... simply imagine earning that kind of money. It's unlikely that you'll know right now how you're going to earn that amount of money — as a matter of fact, at this point, I am certain you don't know how, otherwise you'd already be doing it. But, instead of thinking about 'how' or dismissing the idea as impossible, for now, just pretend it is possible and think about how good it would feel to be earning that kind of money."*

With closed eyes, a schoolgirl smile spread across her face. She loved the idea.

In the moment when she imagined something different, something better for herself, something far beyond any past experience she could compare it to, the decorator's mind had been stretched to a new dimension. Suddenly a doorway had opened up in her mind that invited more income into her life, and this new notion caused her to feel discomfort.

I explained that more one-on-one time with clients wasn't the answer for her. Instead I suggested other ways for her to multiply her income without adding any additional work hours to her schedule.

The reason she had initially recoiled at the idea of exponentially increasing her income was that all of her past thinking and past experience had been challenged. A different kind of reality had been presented, which didn't match what she knew to be real.

Doing something new and different can be a scary thing, yet it's important to understand that fear can play a role in the process of change, and you must work through it. Fortunately, with this awareness, you get to decide whether this fear plays a major or minor role.

Joseph Campbell said it best: *"The cave you fear to enter holds the treasure that you seek."*

Fortunately, I was able to get her to see not only what was holding her back, but also the possibilities available to her on the other side of the fear were limitless. At the conclusion of our meeting, I had a plan for a beautifully decorated home, and she had an exciting future ahead of her and she was now focused on her new demands.

Engage your imagination
in the possibility of new possibilities.

Be willing to step forward into growth.

When Michelangelo was sculpting the statue of David, people would often stop by the studio to see the progress. One day, a father visited with his son at a point when David's form was visible in the piece of marble.

"How did you know he was in there?" the little boy asked.

Michelangelo pondered the question a moment, then replied, *"Every block of stone has a statue inside it, and it is the sculptor's job to discover it. I saw the angel in the marble and carved until I set him free."*

I think Michelangelo's words illustrate the process perfectly. He used his imagination to see an angel's figure in the solid block of rock, then he set his tools to work, and chipped away at it until he sculpted a masterpiece. He first saw the finished sculpture on the screen of his mind, held the vision and took action, then David came to life.

Another example is Walt Disney. Initially, he made animated films, and ended up creating a magnificent empire filled with must-buy merchandise and must-visit destinations like Disneyland and Disneyworld and multiple revenue streams within his business. At the start, he glimpsed the potential of all of it in his mind. You have the same ability, the same equipment and the same "humanness" to do as the trailblazers who came before you did.

Being a creator of your own life is much the same process for anyone who has ever achieved anything of importance. You have that same power within you. You can create incredible things. And, since you're going to create something anyway, make it bold and beautiful and do it consciously and with intention. Don't settle for the small stuff. Think BIG! Make it be something you have no earthly idea how it's going to happen. There is inspiration in pursuing your deepest desires.

Imagine for a moment that your mind is a garden, and in its soil, you can grow anything you want. You plant your ideas in it like seeds and watch them grow. Your thoughts are your garden's water; the images you hold are its sun; and the belief in its attainment – along with all the emotions you sprinkle in – are the nutrients. Positive, productive emotions are like vitamins ... whereas any negative, destructive emotions are like poison.

Exercise:

Revisit your list of demands, adding new ideas to it as they present themselves and subtracting from it those things which don't feel right, or you no longer want.

Organize your list of demands. Order each demand in priority order from most important to least important. Rearrange them until they feel right.

This list of demands is now your Garden of Desires.

{ "All our dreams can come true,
if we have the courage
to pursue them."
- *Walt Disney* }

BELIEVE

PART TWO

Chapter Six
How To Build Faith

In Part One: Conceive, you invested time defining your desires, imagining your big dreams, and converting them into demands…demands that you have no idea how they're going to come about. Many people won't take any steps or make any moves in the direction of their demands until they know the "how." I promise that you don't have to know the "how" to take your imaginings from your mind and begin putting them on solid footing. Think of it like building a house: the process starts with a desired outcome and/or design, and then plans are created and the work begins … one brick at a time.

In Part Two: Believe, I am going to introduce you to an effective, proven tool that will help to build your belief. These are techniques that I have incorporated into my everyday life that have helped me to successfully achieve my demands.

Jim Rohn, the personal development guru said it best:

"Success is nothing more than a few simple disciplines, practiced every day."

If you'd like to have more, be more and do more, I encourage you to pay close attention to the activities I am going to show you. Because if you make a habit of doing them daily, they will keep your demands in front of you, helping you to stay on track.

Oftentimes, people give up on their dreams, not because they don't want them to happen, but because they tend to lose focus or as they experience obstacles, they take that as a "sign" it isn't working and stop the flow. In order to avoid making that simple mistake, follow through on all the exercises, stay the course and make the committed decision to do whatever it takes to realize your demands.

Give yourself a command and follow through on it.

Stay focused.

You must DEMAND this of yourself.

Someone once asked me the following wonderful question — *"What does the average day look like for Peggy McColl?"*

There are a number of things I do every single day with total commitment that keep me moving toward my demands. I call them my Daily Disciplines. In fact, I have done them now for so long that my life would feel "off" if I skipped even a single day. And, of course, I never skip a day. Never ever ever (ever!)

– not even on holidays. I love to say, *"Our dreams don't take vacations!"*

These are specific things that take me in the direction of my demands and keep me focused on their attainment; knowing in my heart that my demands have already manifested into form. My Daily Disciplines are as follows:

- **List of Demands** - I review my written list of demands and update it on a regular basis, removing things that have been accomplished, and adding to the list new demands that pop into my mind.

- **Power Life Script®** - I have written out a description of the life I most desire, in the present tense as if it has already happened, and I have recorded it in my own voice. I listen to it several times each day and update it regularly. This literally re-programs my sub-conscious mind with the beliefs and the knowing that my dream life is already mine and I feel it naturally. *(This is the most powerful tool I have ever used, and it works like magic to manifest my every demand!)*

- **Demand Card** - I carry my written demand (my top priority demand) in my purse or in my pocket everywhere I go. I look at it often throughout the day and connect to the feeling of the demand, as if it has already been accomplished.

- **Gratitude Journal** - Upon waking, every day faithfully, I write what I have in my life that I am grateful for. I count my blessings. I include things that are not currently in my life and I include things that are already in my life. For the future demands, I experience the genuine feeling of gratitude, connecting to these demands as if they are already here.

- **Affirmations** - I read aloud positive statements that support me and build the necessary beliefs.

- **Mirror work** - I look at myself lovingly in the mirror and affirm just how worthy and deserving I am.

- **Visualization** - I invest time imagining how wonderful it feels now that my demands are realized, and I am filled with gratitude that it has already happened.

For nearly four decades, I have prioritized the above activities and made them habits, because they have worked wonders in my life. The results have so astounded me that I keep doing them. Doing them daily has built my belief in attaining any demand I set my mind to.

I truly believe anyone can accomplish any demand they set for themselves. No one could have predicted from my modest upbringing that I would grow up to now be living such an extraordinary, fulfilling and abundant life. The whole reason I wanted to write this book was to share with you the power of these daily disciplines that I repeat faithfully day after day and to show you how simple it can be. But just doing them isn't enough.

Experience has taught me that it's not what you're doing, but *how* you are doing it that matters. It's not enough that you write out your demands, or carry a Demand Card, or listen to a Power Life Script®, or read a great book. To gain the full effect of the Demand Principle, you must perform these exercises daily **with** feeling. You must crank up the power on your feeling output.

Adding emotion to these activities has had the biggest impact on my results and on the results of my clients, and it will certainly have the biggest impact on your results too. It comes down to constant improvement as well. Once you start these disciplines, stay focused on how you can constantly improve upon these activities to enhance the experience.

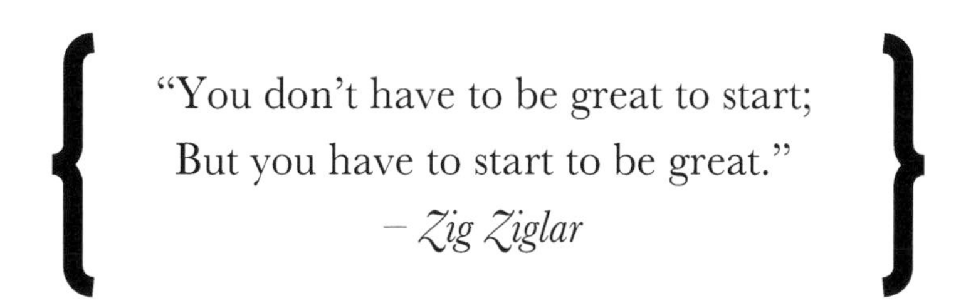

It is important I point out that the things I do every day are all ***feeling state inducements***. For example, writing in my Gratitude Journal puts me into a certain vibration in which I am completely filled with the elated feeling of gratitude for all the good I already have in my life and the good that is coming my way.

Every morning, I enthusiastically grab my Gratitude Journal that sits in the top drawer of my nightstand. The first thing I do is write in it. I write not only simple things that I'm grateful for, like waking up to another beautiful day or being thankful for having good health, but I've learned how important it is to also include powerful feelings like joy, faithfulness and whatever it happens to be so I'm overflowing with positive emotion.

I also read several pages of affirmations to support my pursuits and elevate the self-concept I have of myself. However, I can't expect to get great results by simply reading them. One could read affirmations all day long without emotion, and it would be like reading a telephone book—a stranger's name followed by an unfamiliar number.

You can, however, expect great results when you religiously connect on a **deeply personal and emotional level**. You must feel the accomplishment of your demand, to the point that it feels natural.

Recently, someone asked me if I listen to my Power Life Script® actively. *"Yes and no,"* I said. *"I listen to it both actively and passively."* Repetition of the feeling states is the key.

When I am actively listening, I'm consciously aware of seeing the image in my mind and feeling how it feels in my body. When I am passively listening, the recording plays in the background on low volume, which helps to cement those ideas into my sub-conscious mind ... I may not be consciously aware, but nonetheless, the deposits are being made. The more you activate your emotions, the better you're going to feel about listening to your Power Life Script®.

Throughout the day, I often stop and ask myself, *"Now that my desire is fulfilled, how do I feel?"* As I ask myself this question, I actively connect to my highest priority demand... the one on my Demand Card... and vividly see it and feel it as if it has already come to pass. I would suggest you write out that question and refer to it often throughout the day, too.

Now that your desire is fulfilled,
how do you feel?

Here is a little more distinction around what you see as it relates to a demand. First off, you must absolutely decide what you want. You should absolutely have your demands defined in writing before proceeding. So if you haven't done that already or if you've been hesitant to write down your demands or if you're not sure that you have the “right” demands, I recommend that you invest some time now into sitting down and getting clear on what your demands are, making sure that you are **in love** with them.

Refer back to the Desire—Decide—Dedicate—Demand process in Chapter One; I suggest you do it now. Your future self will thank you!

Be in love with your demands.

Decide what you would love most of all in life, remembering that you do NOT need to know how you're going to get there; just decide that you want it.

Let's assume for a moment that you have decided what you would love. The next step is to become so clear on it that you know exactly what it looks like and how it feels now that the demand has manifested into form. Ask yourself, *“What does it feel like when I'm doing that or have that or am that?”*

During a conversation with a client recently, I asked her what her big demand was. I could immediately tell her desire hadn't yet become a demand because she wasn't really connected to it. Her goal still needed to cross the threshold into the realm of a demand … she didn't yet know with certainty that it would come about.

In an effort to get her wish to the "demand" level, I asked her the following questions:

- *"What does it that look like now that you're doing that?"*
- *"How does it feel now that you've achieved your demand?"*
- *"Describe the picture, but more importantly and most importantly, describe how you feel now that your demand has manifested in your life."*

This exercise helped her become very clear on what she really wanted, and when it had been infused with enough faith and belief, I saw the expression on her face change once she had connected with it.

Ask yourself these above questions often – they will help to reinforce your demands. They will also help you get into alignment with the goods you desire.

Once you connect to the feeling — the "knowing" that you have the power to manifest anything — then you allow the laws of the universe do the rest. Of course, you will be taking the action to bring about your demand as well, but be sure to infuse feeling into the equation because the magical recipe is not "only" action or "only" tapping into Universal Law. I can say with complete confidence that I wouldn't be experiencing the success that I am experiencing if I had never taken action. It's the combination of physical and spiritual action that manifests.

You must take action — massive action — to live the life of your dreams.

All action is not equal. Taking personal responsibility for your actions every day is imperative for the realization of your demands. And honestly… sometimes "corrective action" is needed. When things are not working the way you would have liked, when things go sideways, or when something unexpected occurs in your life, remain open and flexible. Whether you interpret an event as negative or positive, it brings with it an opportunity: the opportunity to course correct; to put yourself back on track.

Do not allow yourself to get down, to go into the negative — don't sweat it. Just like the book title suggests: *"Don't Sweat The Small Stuff, And It's All Small Stuff."*

Return to the ideal place in your mind, to that clear picture of your demand accomplished; combine it with positive emotional feelings, and relax in the knowing that it is already done – **it was done the moment you demanded it.**

Inspired action will naturally spring forth f thoughts and feelings you hold in your mind and he certainty of attaining your demand will pull you along you into doing whatever action necessary for your de come about. Often, you'll get an idea for an action you seemingly from "thin air"; a lot of people like to descr as "downloads from the Universe". This will begin to b daily – if not hourly – occurrence for you when you en Demand Principle in your life. *(TIP: If you ever notice happening – simply revert back to this book and bring it back to*

Exercise:

Determine your Daily Disciplines.

Get clear on what you will commit to doing every day that will get you aligned with your demands. Follow the guidance as shared in this chapter and put it into practice today.

"The game is my wife.
It demands loyalty and responsibility
and gives me back fulfillment
and peace."

- *Michael Jordan*

Chapter Seven
See It Done Continuously

The quote that was cited at the end of the previous chapter is from Michael Jordan. Michael was unequivocally one of the greatest athletes of our time. He became a great athlete by demanding more of himself.

He stepped onto the basketball court to win. In addition to demanding more of himself, he demanded more from the game, as a team competition. He demanded more from his team and the coaching staff. His philosophy of life inspired him to continue to get better and he did get better and better.

During his career, Michael Jordan won 6 NBA Championships, earned 14 Most Valuable Player Awards and was selected to 14 All-Star games and was noted as one of the greatest athletes of the century. These are the kinds of results that people who demand more of themselves achieve.

To cement this idea of your demands being hardened into fact, it is essential that when you demand, you blend it with certainty. Mildly wishing or hoping that your demand will come to pass is not enough. You must employ the "Actor's Technique" and "act as if". You must know your demand is already done, and take action as someone who owns their desire does.

Get into the state of mind where you can see your demand in a completed state even before you begin. This invites a relaxed state of mind. You relax in the knowing that your demand is already done. You vividly feel it in the now and see it playing out perfectly on the screen of your mind. This relaxed state activates your creativity, and opens up your connection to the Divine.

As you go along, if you encounter a setback or circumstances which for a moment may make it appear impossible or implausible that you will achieve what you're striving for, stay focused! Return to the feeling of your demand fulfilled. In other words, know that your demand is absolutely guaranteed. In time, all your efforts will have been worth it. You will have whatever it is you demand.

Years ago, my husband and I created a demand for a second home; a waterfront cottage. Following what I teach and preach, I implemented my daily disciplines and began to see us owning and enjoying our new waterfront oasis. In my imagination, I would wake up in this second home and turn my head and see the water. In my imagination, I would go to sleep in our new second home hearing the sounds of the loons. I saw us enjoying multiple boat rides on the lake. I saw the doggies playing in the yard of this waterfront property. I imagined entertaining friends and family at our waterfront home. I watched the sunsets from the deck and felt the warmth of the outdoor fireplace. I tasted the food what we would cook up as we enjoyed the gentle breeze across our faces.

All of this imagining was done in my mind and heart while fully embracing the feeling states associated with this demand, as if it was already fulfilled. I was feeling the reality of this outcome with my senses (hearing, sight, smell, taste, and touch).

Within a relatively short period of time, we found the perfect waterfront cottage and it was located within a 35-minute drive from our main home … and within a few short months, we purchased this second waterfront home, took possession and began to enjoy what was previously only an idea in my imagination. This second home was once a dream, that turned into a demand – and ultimately became a reality.

Feeling is the great secret to everything;

Visualizing while feeling the effects fuels the demand …

And **taking action** creates the results.

By using this dynamic "triple power" combination as a tool, you will feel yourself right to the reality of your demand fulfilled.

"How can I create more vivid images with deeper feeling?"

This is a great question to ask yourself , and the following will help intensify this process for you.

When you are enhancing your visualization experience, think in terms of V.A.K. (Visual, Auditory and Kinesthetic). You want to See, Hear, and Smell/Taste/Touch your desire inside your imagination.

In other words, what do you see – now that your demand is fulfilled? What do you hear – now that your demand is fulfilled? What do you feel – now that your demand is already fulfilled?

Invite all of your senses to be a part of this vividly imagined reality.

Use visualization to intensify those feelings.

The other evening my husband and I were watching a television show based on real events where a gentleman was convicted of a crime that he said he did not do.

The man seemed very sincere. The detectives didn't believe him, because all the physical evidence pointed to his guilt, so they gave him a polygraph test. The gentleman agreed to take it and passed the polygraph test.

The detectives still weren't convinced, so they decided to run the test again. The gentleman passed again. Still, they didn't believe him.

Over and over, the detectives put the gentleman through one test after another, phrasing the questions differently, and hoping to catch him in a lie. But the gentleman kept passing the test.

Eventually, the real criminal came forward and confessed to the crime, which finally got the detectives to believe the gentleman's innocence.

Why did the gentleman pass the polygraph test? Because he was innocent, and he knew it. His belief in the truth was so rock solid that he answered the detective's questions with unwavering conviction about his innocence. There wasn't one shred of doubt in his mind about whether he was innocent.

You may be wondering why I'm sharing this story about the man and the polygraph test. During a polygraph test, electrodes are attached to various points on a person's body to monitor physical reactions, such as blood pressure, pulse, respiration and skin conductivity, to questions … and these reactions will determine whether the responses given to the questions are true or false. Now, think about your demand for a moment…

How convinced are you that your demand will come to pass?

The level of your conviction about the outcome you desire must be so high that you believe it to your core. If you took a polygraph test and were asked if you believed you would attain your demand, would you pass?

How would you respond? How would your body react? Would the machine detect a wavering belief? How strong is your belief?

A polygraph is able to tell whether you're sincere or not when asked certain questions. Although polygraphs aren't 100% accurate, they are in most cases. However, there are people who know how to fool them.

They fool them by believing so strongly in their answers with 100% certainty that their bodies never show the presence of a negative thought; never display a negative reaction and never doubt their conviction to the truth.

This is the sort of conviction you must have when you are visualizing your demand. It must feel true and real. If you're lying or you feel like you're lying, you are out of alignment with your dream.

Make sure you're in alignment.

In this instance, it is not about fooling anyone; It is about mentally, emotionally, spiritually and physically becoming your demand.

There certainly will be times when you get off track – Everybody gets off track. Your job is to recognize when it happens, then just put yourself back on track as quickly as possible… and with all of this awareness, you can do it quicker than most.

One of my close friends decided it was time to make a change, so she committed to getting in shape again. The demand she set for herself was to release a hundred pounds of excess weight.

She demanded of herself to be disciplined enough to stick to a few new habits to reach her desired weight. She spent time imagining her slimmer self, feeling how good it would feel to be walking around in her tight-fitting jeans, going to the swimming pool in her new swimsuit, enjoying the smaller portions of delicious food, and exercising every day. Then she did it.

She had made the promise to herself and followed through on her actions. Consistently and vigorously, the weight melted away. It had to – she **demanded** it!

At first, it may feel like your demand is a lie, because it isn't "real" in your life…but it is real in your imagination. Everything begins in the mind. Focus on the mental reality for now; Stick with it and feed your conviction with the positive that it will soon be "real" in your life as it is now in your Through the Demand Principle, you will create it.

Exercise:

Demand Card

Write out your most important demand on a demand card (a piece of paper about the size of a business card). Write the demand statement as if the demand has already been accomplished (present tense using positive words only).

Throughout the day, read your demand and meditate on it. Look at it often. Feel what it would feel like if it had already come to pass. Let your mind go to the place that Thomas Edison called "The Land of Solutions" — an infinite storehouse of knowledge and possibility.

This is where your imagination, in the most positive way, sees and emotionalizes your demands as if they have already materialized in your world.

My Demand

I am so happy and grateful now that

____

____

____

www.PeggyMcColl.com

Peggy McColl

New York Times Best Selling Author

"I don't dream at night,
I dream all day;
I dream for a living."
- *Steven Spielberg*

Chapter Eight

The Revision Process

Everyone talks to themselves, whether they realize it or not. Chances are high that right now a voice in your head is talking to you. What is the voice saying? Is it being kind and supportive? Is it positive, encouraging and uplifting? Or, is it being negative and non-supportive?

For some strange reason, humans are generally conditioned to think and feel negative. And, for another reason more bizarre than the first, humans aren't generally aware of the internal dialogue that is playing in the background of their mind like a soundtrack of their lives.

This voice is like a recording that plays the same song on a scratched record, repeating the same old thing and bringing about the same old results. Oftentimes, complaints, defeats and past mistakes are repeated as if the Sunday Night Football's instant replay mode on our televisions was stuck on a perpetual repeat cycle.

What we say to ourselves in our heads plays a role in shaping our behavior, our self-perception and, ultimately, the results we see in our lives. Sadly, most people aren't aware that there is a voice in there, let alone are they aware of what it is saying. With practice, everyone can change what they say to themselves.

Listening to what you tell yourself
takes self-awareness;
changing it takes discipline.

Take a moment right now to listen to that voice inside your head.

"What voice?", you ask?

The one that just asked, *"What voice?"*. :-)

Become aware of the thoughts that you are thinking about yourself, and if you catch that voice saying something other than a supportive thought, change the recording to one that is positive and uplifting. Recreate every scenario in your mind in a way that serves you and makes you feel good and has you connecting only to the good that you desire. In fact, you can revise any experience you've encountered: the events of an entire day, situations at work, test results…whatever you desire.

This is something Neville Goddard talks about, and it is known as The Revision Process. You can revise events and see them in your minds' eye the way you want them to manifest.

You can revise your day and see it only as you desire it to be. You can revise anything in your imagination.

As an example, let's pretend you've just started a business, and one of the services you desire to provide to the world is a show where you interview experts on a specific topic. You're new in the business, so no one knows you yet, but you send out twenty invitations to experts who you'd love to interview on your show. As the day goes on, most of them don't respond to you; And the ones who do say, *"Thanks, but no thanks."*

In this scenario, you have a choice; you can feel defeated, down and discouraged, or you can deny those negative emotions from impacting you. Inside your imagination, you can close your eyes and imagine that everyone responded positively to your invitations, and you're booking interviews rapidly. You imagine how it feels to be building the business of your dreams and impacting millions of people with these show episodes alone.

Doing this revision process will keep you in the game and on the way to manifesting your demand. Your energetic vibration – thoughts, feelings and emotions – will remain positive, and you will continue taking positive action the next day, producing productive results.

Life is really just a game, and it can be very fun game if we demand it to be.

Frankly, if life is not fun, then you're not doing it right.

You might ask, *"But how do I win at the game of life?"*

The answer is simple: feed your dream. Instead of focusing on what you don't have, or what didn't happen, give your dream positive energy.

If you've been in debt, stop giving the debt any negative thought or emotional energy. Instead, see your financial situation the way you would love for it to be, and feel it in the present tense as if you are already financially abundant. Take actions, such as creating an automated payoff plan that eliminates the debt without you having to give it another thought – and only focus on what you really want. Begin to imagine that you could do, be and have whatever it is you want in life. Nothing can stop you.

Remember, you have the power to take control of your thinking now!

Start using your imagination to record a new internal dialogue to play out in your mind. Anytime you notice emotions like worry, doubt, fear, anxiousness or anger creeping in, go back to that new soundtrack of your ideal dream life and/or situation and feel/act as if it is already here!

Whenever anything comes up like an echo in your head and it doesn't feel good, it sabotages your results. The negative thoughts are adding fuel to other negative beliefs. Get out of your own way, stop the insanity, and follow the Demand Principle, staying focused on the best possible outcome you want.

This may take some time, but through repetition and steady awareness you can change this. You must consciously notice the chatter, then override it with positive statements of encouragement. Simply notice what's happening in your mind, return to the good feeling of how wonderful it is now that your demand has been fulfilled ,and turn on the positive thought and feeling waterfall.

I recall many years ago when my accountant had completed my income tax submission. He emailed me to tell me how much tax I owed. I was anticipating having to pay taxes and had calculated a rough estimate in my head. But when the email arrived in my inbox, I was shocked at the amount outstanding. It was significantly higher than I had anticipated, and, upon reading the email and reviewing the documents, I was feeling a great sense of panic. The first question that popped in my mind was, *"How am I going to pay this?"*

Immediately recognizing that panic is a destructive emotional state, I switched my focus and asked myself an empowering question: *"What would you love, Peggy?"*

The answer was easy – *"To see and know my taxes are all paid up and paid in full"*. I chose to focus on knowing that all taxes were paid up and paid in full. I felt what it would feel like to have this accomplished; in fact, I demanded it paid in full and with ease.

The due date for the tax payment was only a few weeks away, but I maintained my positive outlook and saw the end result, as I desired. Within a couple of days, an idea sparked in my mind and I moved into action. I demanded more of myself. I demanded that I earn the additional funds and that I would do it relatively quickly. The Universe loves speed.

So, I speedily moved into action. By revising my feelings and embracing the sense of certainty that this demand was accomplished, everything fell into place; I created and launched a new online program and the taxes were paid up and paid in full.

Another example of the revision process occurred a few years ago for one of my private mentoring clients. A client was writing a book with a co-writer and both parties were making significant contributions to their book. Halfway through the project, her writing partner suddenly cut off all communication with the outside world. At first, my client was concerned, and then as more time passed with no communication, she got angry. She mentally rehearsed and prepared herself for a legal battle. She asked me, *"What do I do now?"*

"What would you love?" I asked. *"Ask yourself this important question: 'What would I love as an outcome?' What scenario would be ideal for you?"*

In her response, she kept talking about conflict, conflict, conflict.

As gently as possible I told her the following. *"Stop creating in your mind a worst-case scenario and reimagine the best-case scenario.* ***There's never conflict where harmony exists.*** *Envision a perfect unfoldment as you wish the events to unfold... now, tell me about that."*

After thinking for a moment, she took a deep breath, released the conflict and began describing a benevolent outcome between her and the other writer.

"Great!" I said, *"Now, only give positive energy to that. Be grateful that the ideal outcome you'd like to experience has happened, and act as if it has come to pass."*

We got to work writing down affirming statements for her to repeat to herself. She went to work thinking only positively about the situation. Whenever that voice began going down "Negative Street", she caught herself and repeated her affirmations.

About a month later, she called me up and said, *"You're not going to believe it, but we reached an agreement without a legal battle. I am amazed how well this process worked."* The conflict had resolved itself harmoniously without a legal battle, because she had mentally conditioned her mind to expect a benevolent outcome.

With practice and awareness, you can pay attention to what you're paying attention to. Start becoming aware of what saying to yourself; be kind and supportive instead of ıg yourself or others down. Without judgement, observe houghts and when you find one that doesn't serve you, ate it by replacing it with something better.

Revise your thinking. Revise your events with your ıation. Discipline yourself to change the dialogue you to yourself on a continual basis. You'll love the effects.

Exercise:

Affirmations

Avoid possible self-confusion by proactively and consciously catching yourself when you have negative or destructive thoughts and speak your positive affirmations to yourself.

With your increased self-awareness, notice when you're talking to yourself negatively or you're being unkind toward yourself or others. When you spot this, catch it and then simply switch. You force yourself to switch your thinking from the negative to the positive.

Keep reading your demands three times a day, reprioritizing them until the order feels perfect. With consistency, an affirming dialogue will emerge as your dominant internal dialogue.

{ “The more man meditates
upon good thoughts,
the better will be his world
and the world at large.”
- *Confucius* }

Chapter Nine

Cause And Effect

Emerson said that the "law of all laws" is the law of cause and effect. Newton's third law states that for every action, there is an equal and opposite reaction. The Bible says, as you sow, so shall you reap. All of these words of wisdom basically say the same thing:

Everything you do will cause something else to happen.

- Turn on the faucet (cause), and water will flow forth (effect).
- Flip on the light switch (cause), light will fill the room (effect).
- Focus on the good you have (cause), better will show up into your life (effect).

As simple as this law is to comprehend, most people overlook the importance of it. Maybe you dismissed when your grandmother told you to count your blessings. Or, perhaps, you ignored a friend's recommendation to be grateful for the things you have. The magic locked up within this law will be unleashed with the practice of gratitude.

Being grateful fixes your mind on the good things you have in your life, and according to the law, good will come back to you.

So how grateful are you?

To concentrate your thoughts on negative things will lead you to be negative and attract to you negative experiences. On the other hand, if you focus your attention on positive and inspiring thoughts, they will attract to you positive and inspiring experiences, and you will be positive and inspiring. It all goes back to the law of cause and effect.

You are a powerful magnet.
The energy you send out,
be it positive or negative,
will always come back to you.

Over the course of the past four decades that I have studied personal development, I can say unequivocally that one of the disciplines which has made the biggest difference in my life for the attainment of my demands and the peace and happiness I enjoy has been the practice of gratitude.

Being grateful fixes the mind's energy upon the goodness that exists all around, and it attracts more of that goodness to the one who is grateful. Gratitude puts one closer to the source from which all goodness springs. When you focus your awareness on that good, it sets you upon the frequency that attracts to you more of the same, and better results will be attracted to you.

Besides, it is impossible to feel bad when you're grateful.

Be filled with delight for the blessings you've already received, and more blessings will rain down upon you.

The practice of gratitude puts you in harmony with the good you desire. When you do, you open the door for more of it to flow into your life.

Each morning when I wake up, I grab my gratitude journal and begin writing what I am grateful for. I revel in the thought of the things that bring happiness and joy into my life, even the simplest of things I find worthy of being grateful for—hot water in the shower, a comfortable bed, the love and support from those whom I am closest to — for these are the best things in my life — and I am grateful for all of them. Then, I hold that feeling and imagine my demand.

I imagine that it has already come about, that it's already here. I am grateful to already be in possession of it. Even if it only exists in my mind. I act as if it exists for real…because it does!

Thoughts are things and everything all around you existed first in someone's mind. The chair you're sitting in, the car you're driving, the glass you drink from, all of these things were once nothing more than ideas.

Be happy and grateful for the attainment of your dream as if your dream has already come to pass in your life.

Here are examples of some gratitude statements I have previously written in my gratitude journal:

- *"I'm so happy and grateful now that I own and live in our spacious, first-class, spectacular and beautifully decorated home."*
- *"I am so happy and grateful now that each member of my family and every one of my friends is experiencing perfect health and happiness."*
- *"I am so happy and grateful now that money comes to me in increasing quantities from multiple sources on a continuous basis."*

Doing this makes the reality of it feel REAL. I do this so much with everything that thinking positively about my demands has become a habit. It is a learned behavior, cultivated over time. I wouldn't go a day without writing in my gratitude journal. I have done it so long that it is now a habitual behavior for me.

People who continue to create or recreate what they don't want, have fallen into an endless cycle … a pattern, a rhythm that they'll stay in forever ***unless and until*** they gain the awareness that what they're doing is causing them to get the same results year after year.

If they paid attention and began to shift their focus from the negative to the positive things in life, it would put them in vibration with the source from which all the good they desire comes. And they would begin to invite bigger, better and happier experiences into their lives.

The act of being grateful automatically puts you into a state to receive more, and the simple act of writing down what you're grateful for energizes your mindset to attract to you what you demand.

Exercise:

Gratitude Journal

Begin keeping a Gratitude Journal. Every morning when you wake up, write down what you are grateful for.

To make it a habit, place your Gratitude Journal on your bedside table.

It doesn't matter if it is loose leaf paper, a yellow legal pad, or a leather-bound notebook — any sort of notepad will do.

Jot down at least ten things that you are grateful for.

"Piglet noticed that even though he had a Very Small Heart, it could hold a rather large amount of Gratitude."

- A.A. Milne

PART THREE

ACHIEVE

Chapter Ten
Repetition Is Key

The expression "practice makes perfect" proves to be true, because the more you do something, the better at it you become if and when "better" is what you are focusing on.

How did you learn your name? The first time your parents called you by your name, you certainly didn't understand that the sound of the word referred to you. How could you? You were just a baby. The recognition that your name referred to you was only understood after hearing it over and over for a long period of time. All things are learned through repetition.

Repetition is one of the secrets to success. It's the key to everything, really. When you hear a song enough times, you learn the lyrics; when you practice a dance routine enough, you learn the sequence of spins, steps and twirls; and, when you hear your name repeated over the course of time, you learn it and you respond to it. With the simple understanding of the power of repetition, you can master anything when you repeat it often enough.

How is a habit formed? Through repetition! Nearly everything you do is a habit, and you came about forming each of your habits by performing them over and over until you mastered them, and they became second nature.

The only way to change an already-established habit is through focus, determination and repetition. You must **demand** yourself to change a habit, or replace an old one with a new one. Follow the four-step Demand Principle process and watch what happens.

Now, let's talk about *The Three Phases of Changing A Behavior*. Chances are you will initially fall in love with the idea of incorporating these new Daily Disciplines into your life, but you may experience challenges. So, let's look at things from a birds-eye view to eliminate those challenges.

The Three Phases of Changing A Behavior:

1) **Infatuation** - In this first phase, you want a change in your life so much that you will begin with enthusiasm.

2) **Reality Check** - In this second phase, reality sets in. It will soon become clear that your old way of doing things is changing and your paradigm (the old way of doing things) won't want you to change. It will fight and struggle with you

at every turn to regain and retain control, so you will have to persevere and assert power over it in order to "slay the beast." Perseverance, determination, and willpower, with a focus to realize the changes you desire to experience in your life, will be the weapons in your arsenal to move on to the final phase. This is where the Demand Principle will really allow you to shine.

3) **Second Nature** - In this third and final phase, your new habit will be formed. Performing your new habit will seem so commonplace, so natural that you won't even think about it anymore; you'll just do it. The reason why so many people fail is because they never get to this all-important third stage. They didn't activate the power of the Demand Principle and allowed their desire to fade.

Years ago, I started working with a woman who was unhappy with her finances. She faced a mountain of debt and her internal dialogue, using her own words, *"was making her sick"*. She said, *"Just thinking about going to the mailbox makes me want to throw up."*

"That is your choice," I said.

"You are always in control of how you feel, whether you realize it or not. I have a question for you: How does thinking like that serve you?" I asked with a smile on my face yet voiced it in a serious tone.

"Thinking that way just recreates more of the same undesirable experiences to come into your life. What if you changed your attitude about your bills? What if you went to the mailbox, and when you received a bill, you paid it with a deep sense of gratitude?"

My words startled her into identifying a long-held paradigm probably learned from observation in her childhood when she witnessed her parent's constant struggle with money. At this discovery, her reaction was palpable. It only took her a minute to realize that her focus had been misdirected. I got her to shift her thinking from one of displeasure when paying for her bills to one of being grateful for the services that had been provided her.

Focus on the service you receive
and pay for it graciously.

Then I really rocked her world. "*What if you switched your attitude to one of excitement when you go to the mailbox?"* I asked.

"How would you feel if you were suddenly getting big checks in the mail, or what if you received a statement from your bank confirming a big payout on returns from your investments?"

"I'd love that!" She said excitedly.

"I'd run to the mailbox every day."

"Live in that good feeling all the time," I said, encouragingly. *"Tell yourself how much you love money, and that you easily attract it into your life. You will soon recognize it as being true."*

Like everything else that you are discovering in this book, you have to tap into your imagination and feel the feelings sincerely and consistently. This process is not rocket science, it simply requires awareness and repetition. We are talking about simple, practical methods that you can apply immediately; and/but you must apply them over and over again.

Over time and through repetition, my client was able to turn her financial ship around. Now she has a healthy approach to money and loves going to the mailbox and she is enjoying a healthier financial outcome.

Every single day I do certain things that take me in the direction my demands and more importantly I live FROM my demands (meaning – my demands are already accomplished in my mind and in my heart). These "certain things" that I do every day are the Daily Disciplines that I outlined in Chapter Six: How To Build Faith.

I write in my gratitude journal, read my affirmations, listen to my Power Life Script®, visualize my demands while feeling positive emotions and imagine them as if they've already come to pass, read my Demand Card and my Demand Plaque (more on this in a moment), I do my mirror work… You see, it isn't a "one and done" proposition; It's the doing of them **every day** that holds the magic.

When you incorporate these Daily Disciplines into your life, and repeat them every day, I guarantee you will see a dramatic change in your life in a very short amount of time and these disciplines will begin to be habits for you as you'll naturally move into action every single day.

Repetition gives your Daily Disciplines the power to transform your life.

I have a client who loves to sing. Ever since she was a child, she sang, and to this day, it remains the passion of her life. Her big dream is to win a Grammy.

One day when I was helping her to connect to her big demand, bridging the gap between her current reality and the life she'd love to experience, I told her, *"Imagine you are a successful singer and everywhere you go people recognize you. In fact, you're so famous that you can't even go to the restroom without people bombarding you for autographs and selfies. Practice feeling this feeling every day. Go to the grocery store in disguise. Put a scarf over your head, wear sunglasses and pretend you're experiencing the sort of recognition that Lady Gaga or Madonna might experience when they go out shopping. You want to live as if it is already true."*

Recently, she told me that the grocery store exercise helped her to truly connect with her lifelong dream. Now, she sings in clubs, records in studios and writes and performs her own songs all while she still goes to the grocery store in disguise.

It's the repetitive doing of these things that fuels her desire and stirs her to take action in the direction of her big demand. All of this may sound silly, until you try it for yourself – and notice that it works.

If you love the idea of having, being and doing more in life, then I suggest you get a sign made up — a ***Demand Plaque*** — with an amount of money that you demand of the universe. Remember to stretch yourself, similar to the story you read earlier in this book about the salesmen who visited the business owner's office. Come up with a number that's big, something that really scares you and excites you at the same time... Because it takes the same amount of energy to manifest a hundred dollars as it does to manifest a million. Your sign might read something like this:

"I Demand My Personal Annual Income To Be $12,000,000!"

One word of caution... It's not enough to just tap into your imagination and conjure up an idea in your mind and wait. That's just dreaming.

Dreaming is great, but dreaming alone will not call it forth. The picture of your demand must be anchored in with the ***feeling***, a feeling of CERTAINTY, joy and happiness as if your dream is already here. And, you must take action from this feeling state.

Any time and every time you are not feeling as if that demand is already here, you are not in alignment with your demand. You are not connecting to it, and, consequently, it is not a powerful productive positive state to be in. You are very likely going to hit an invisible wall, and the fulfillment of your demand will be waiting on the other side of the barrier. It is where your freedom lies.

Freedom is where you want to get to. But it's going to take work, effort, increased awareness, time and repetition. Know that it not only works, it works like magic. So, just do it! Time is going to pass anyway; make the most of it and demand the best from yourself – for your own benefit, and the benefit of others.

> "Success is nothing more than
> a few simple disciplines,
> practiced every day."
> - *Jim Rohn*

Exercise:

Demand Plaque

Choose the most exciting demand you have listed and have a Demand Plaque made.

It should read, "I DEMAND _____."

Fill in the blank with that demand as if it is already done, i.e. "*I demand my income is $xxxxxxxxx this year.*"

You could find a custom sign shop online and order it to be delivered to your home. Once it arrives, hang it somewhere you'll see it often i.e. a wall, bathroom mirror or on the ceiling above your bed.

Look at it often and let it inspire you, knowing that the more you think about it, the sooner it will come to pass.

Repeatedly reading your plaque and imagining the feeling of it being true will solidify it in your mind and bring it about in your life.

Chapter Eleven
Flexibility Is Essential To Success

Life's only real inevitability is change. Whoever said it was death and taxes should have looked a little bit deeper. Before governments taxed citizens, change existed, and after death, bodies decomposed. Everything in the universe is in a constant state of change.

All new things are born out of energy transmuting into a new expression of itself. Ice melts to water—water heats to steam — steam becomes ether — it's all the same energy, changing into different forms. It is a universal reality explained in The Law of Perpetual Transmutation — *everything moves, nothing rests.*

The only thing we can truly count on, then, is change. Since this is the case, why do so many people resist change in their lives if it's going to happen anyway? It's time to shift our thinking.

Transform your approach to change.
Embrace change as an opportunity.

You have a choice in how you approach change.

Several years ago, a client of mine, Elle Newmark, an aspiring author who had written a couple of books, wanted a book deal with a traditional publisher. She submitted her manuscript, as this was the protocol with traditional publishers back then, and time after time it was rejected. Frustration set in.

"There must be a different way," she said to herself.

In order to get her work out into the world, she knew she would have to take a new approach and find a different way. She contacted me to get my help with leveraging the power of the Internet to effectively launch and self-publish her book.

As a fiction writer, she soon understood that the same methods for launching a book applied to either fiction or non-fiction. She was an excellent student who followed all my recommendations, but she also added her own creative twist to the mix. One such creative action was sending out more than 400 emails to publishers and literary agents the day before her book release to encourage them to watch her book rise up the charts.

The next day, her book took off like a rocket and became an International Best-Seller on Amazon. Within a few days, she signed with a literary agent who put her book up for auction.

Then two weeks later, publishers were bidding to purchase the literary rights to her book.

A large publisher preempted all other bids by offering her a seven-figure publishing deal.

Once Elle realized she would have to break the mold, she went searching for answers. She found a different way and dove headfirst into it. In the end, her dream came true when publishers were clamoring for her book. **Elle had demanded it.**

**Decide on a new approach
and get a new result.**

**Remember this:
there is always a way when
one is committed.**

Venture to a place you've never gone before. The choice to go there is yours. Focus on the destination rather than the road you'll have to take to get there. The "what" supersedes the "how."

Hold fast to the clear picture of what you want to accomplish and, like the lifting of the fog on a crisp autumn day, out of the haze a way will be shown. It all starts with changing how you approach change and how open to that change you are. I'm not talking about pocket change—I'm talking about real transformation in your life.

You can get the results you've always wanted in your life with a simple committed decision to do things differently than you have ever done them before. **Demand "more" and "better" and "new" of yourself.**

By following the process outlined in the Demand Principle, you will discover how powerful you are. When you know more *about* yourself, you can demand more *of* yourself.

The philosopher and essayist, Ralph Waldo Emerson said, *"The only person you are destined to become is the person you decide to be."*

In order for you to become the person you want to be, you must first decide who that is. You have great potential locked up inside of you; embracing change helps to unleash that greatness.

Exercise:

Power Life Script® - It's time to crystalize your thoughts into physical reality by writing them down in written form—the first stage of manifesting them into physical reality and recording them in a Power Life Script® for you to listen to every day.

First, you played with the invisible "clay" in the workshop of your imagination until you settled upon desires that most interested you. Then you molded those wishes into desires as images—but still, they were only enjoyed by you, conjured in the privacy of your own mind.

Next, they turned into goals and, finally, they hardened into demands. The moment you jotted your wishes down on your list of demands in your very own Garden of Desires, you started a process that will forever change the way you look at your potential and the possibilities available to you.

Now, write out a description of the life you'd love to live as if you are living it now — the dream life you yearn for, a life you see for yourself. Decide who you'd like to become.

Be sure to phrase each sentence in present tense as if it has already come to pass. Ensure that all the tones of reality are included.

Be certain you can see this dream life and that you feel the emotions intensely.

In essence, you're writing a movie script for your life that you can live right now. This is what I call your Power Life Script®.

Once you have written it down, record it in your own voice with lots of enthusiasm and joy and begin listening to the recording of your Power Life Script® more than once a day and watch your life transform before your very eyes.

This one technique has made the biggest difference in my life and in my results. I highly recommend you follow through with this exercise now.

For a complete step by step guide, video tutorials, script templates, audio recordings and advanced trainings, visit the website below to discover the complete Power Life Script® program:

www.PowerLifeScript.com

“The only way to make sense
out of change is to plunge into it,
move with it, and
join the dance.”

- *Alan Watts*

Chapter Twelve
You Are Worthy

Luxuriate in the idea that you deserve to be happy. After all, happiness is an inside job … it's not a destination, but a way of being.

The same goes for self-worth and success. Stop listening to the doubters, the dream stealers, and the neigh-sayers of the world who would have you remain with them in the ranks of the mediocre. In most cases, they aren't consciously trying to hold you back … but nonetheless, if you allow them to influence you, they are.

> "Forgive them, for they know not what they are doing."
> *- Luke 23:34*

One of my daily affirmation is the following…

"I attract success and abundance into my life because that is who I am."

I say this with deep emotional conviction, which impresses it upon my subconscious mind. This is an example of a way of being.

Choose to become the greatest and grandest version of you.

Model successful people who have demanded things like you are now demanding for yourself. Proceed confidently forward along the route that leads to your ideal — the image you have created in your mind with the brushstrokes of your imagination.

Proceed boldly into uncharted waters toward your future. Your dreams exist out there in the "unknown". Yes, success is the pursuit of a destination, but real success occurs when you live as if you are already living your dream life currently.

> "Success is the progressive realization of a worthy ideal."
> - *Earl Nightingale*

It's time to discard the self-defeating beliefs and banish the ghosts of your past — they don't define you. They don't even exist right now in this moment. Release the baggage you've collected along life's journey. Let yesterday strengthen your resolve to create a better tomorrow.

The experiences from your past, whether they were painful or not can serve as inspiration, growth and a positive learning experience. You are worthy of what you pursue, and what you pursue is worthy of you.

Get Demanding!

It's time to put your foot down and demand from yourself the change you want in your life. One time in Tampa, a taxi driver picked me up at the airport and he told me he was fed up with dating. *"I finally decided to settle down,"* he said.

I asked, *"What are you going to do differently in your life to bring that about?"*

"I'm going to church and have a conversation with 'the boys'—that's what I call the apostles," he said. *"I will tell them that I am ready for a relationship and ask for help."*

After explaining the Demand Principle to him, I suggested that instead of asking, he should demand it. *"To have a happy, healthy, loving relationship in your life, you must not settle for second best. You must demand exactly that which you want from life."*

I gave him my email and asked him to provide me with an update as things progress.

A few weeks later, an email from him dropped into my inbox. He explained how he told the boys, *"I did not ask for a relationship. I demanded one."* He followed my advice to implement the Demand Principle.

A week later he met the woman who would eventually become his wife.

Demanding more of yourself is an important step to living full out. Alas, making daring moves may feel risky at first. Taking the risk of believing in yourself is the best risk you can possibly take.

> "The cave you fear to enter
> holds the treasure that you seek."
>
> *–Joseph Campbell*

Build your self-worth.

Napoleon Hill, the author of Think And Grow Rich, spoke about building his own self-belief. When Napoleon agreed to undertake Andrew Carnegie's twenty-year challenge -- with no compensation -- to study the most successful businessmen in the world and create a success formula that all people could learn from, Mr. Carnegie knew he would meet with challenging times and want to quit.

Mr. Carnegie said, *"Write down what I am about to say."* The young Napoleon Hill grabbed a pencil. *"Look in a mirror and say to yourself at least twice a day: 'Andrew Carnegie, I am not only going equal your achievements in life, but I am going to catch you at the post and pass you at the grandstand.'"*

Napoleon dropped his pencil and exclaimed, *"You know very well I'm not going to be able to do that!"*

Mr. Carnegie replied, "*I know you won't*—**unless and until** *you believe it! But if you believe it, you will.*"

Despite his misgivings, fear and sense of unworthiness, Napoleon did, as directed, and built his belief by following Mr. Carnegie's direction. As a result, he went on to create more millionaires than anyone in history by teaching his success formula in *Think And Grow Rich*. Napoleon had a choice... to give his attention to his past and his fears, or give his attention to possibility and demand more of himself.

Believe in yourself and others.

Oftentimes, people have a desire, but they don't actually follow through and go for it. Why? It's because they are in their own way. Beliefs play a role in all manifestations. If someone has a belief that they aren't worthy of success, they will sabotage their results. Feeling unworthy is a debilitating belief.

All negative emotions will dampen, destroy, or slow down progress. Doubt, fear, and worry may become overwhelming when you start to move toward your demands. Conquer them. Simply replace those negative and destructive emotions with positive and empowering emotions. Connect with your vision and anchor it in with feeling, then take action every day toward its attainment. Your future is worth the effort.

Many years ago, I began having thoughts that romantic relationships equaled massive pain. This paradigm was created in response to my upbringing bundled with the emotional impact of experiencing several broken relationships over the years including a divorce from my first husband. Once I caught on to my own misguided thinking, I quickly changed it.

After a period of time of creating a new belief, I began to feel differently about relationships and my potential to have a happy one. I also made a firm decision that it was time for a loving and fulfilling connection with my soulmate. I asked myself, *"What do I need to believe in order to have a loving relationship?"*

I wrote out affirming statements and included them in an updated version of my Power Life Script®. I made a demand for a loving relationship in my life. I connected to the outcome emotionally. I visualized being in a happy, loving and committed relationship.

When my now-husband Denis and I started dating, I remember marveling at how effective it had been to demand a partner with the amazing values and qualities I desired. After all, I deserved it—we both did. I attracted Denis into my life two weeks after I made the demand of the universe. I was pleasantly surprised at how effective this technique works.

Denis and I have been happily married now for many years. I often tell people that I won the lottery of love by attracting Denis into my life. I am so grateful for him and our marriage.

Appreciate yourself and others.

A few years ago, I asked Denis, *"Honey, what do you love most about me?"*

Being the analytical, left-brained guy that he is, he didn't just blurt out the first thing that came to mind—he thought about it for several minutes. Then he said, "*What I love most about you is how much you appreciate me.*" And it is true! I appreciate my husband so much.

Every day I think about how grateful I am to have him in my life, and I tell him all the time. And I feel appreciated by him too. After all, we all just want to feel appreciated. Remember, you get what you give. I created that feeling when I demanded something better for myself from my relationships all those years ago.

One of my affirmations is this: *"I only attract harmonious people and harmonious situations into my life, and I deserve only the best. I am worthy of only the best."*

You deserve to demand the best for yourself too.

"Behavior is the mirror in which everyone shows their image."

- *Johann Wolfgang von Goethe*

Exercise:

Mirror Work

You are worthy of anything you decide to achieve. But how do you build the belief? That's simple!

You must decide you are worth it.

At first, it may feel like you're trying to convince yourself that it's true. But in actuality, you must make the decision that you deserve it and here's how you do it.

Stand in front of a mirror and look yourself in the eye. Repeat something like this: *"I love you. I adore you. I am proud of you. You can have, do and be anything you want. You deserve to have, do and be anything you want."*

You can also say your affirmations aloud to yourself in the mirror. It is a very powerful and confidence building exercise.

The more you do it, the more powerful and confident you become.

Chapter Thirteen
Moving Past Fear

Years before Jim Carrey became a world-renowned actor, he wrote himself a check for $10 million dollars for "acting services rendered" and kept it in his wallet. At night, he would drive up on Mulholland Drive, park his car on a vista overlooking the city of Los Angeles, and remove the check from his wallet. With his eyes closed, he would imagine receiving the check and decide how he would spend it when he finally got it.

This activity caused him to feel as if he was already in possession of the success he sought, that he felt deserving of it. He gave no attention to his past — the hundreds of times he was getting booed off stage, the countless roles he did not get, the long list of rejections he had received — it simply didn't matter.

He was building a vision and applying the necessary feelings and emotional state. He held fast to that vision, visiting it often --- the old, tattered and torn check was proof of that. And — he did one other important thing. He took action.

Repeatedly, he tried out for another audition, he attended acting classes, he did whatever he could to move himself toward the manifestation of his dream — something he knew he would eventually have.

He was in service to his vision, a vision he had created by himself, for himself. Soon, he began landing parts in movies and television shows. His star began to rise. The momentum was gathering speed, and he kept it going by continuously marching onward toward his dream until he received a $10 million check for his starring role in the movie Dumb and Dumber.

At the time, it was the highest salary ever paid to an actor for a starring role in a film. Jim Carrey first did the work in his imagination ... he kept doing it, repetitively, for as long as it took ... he took actions in alignment with his demand ... and it paid off – literally.

Each of us has a great power locked inside that wants to express itself. Many of the most successful people you admire have tapped into it – whether consciously, or unconsciously -- and have reaped the rewards. When you unlock your power, you unleash invisible universal forces, "Angels" if you will, who stand at the ready to aid you in your pursuits.

What Jim Carrey did demonstrates the power – and I have included numerous other examples throughout this book as well. Let our examples fuel your desire to succeed, as well as your belief in the knowing that anything you demand is already done.

Do what you can
from where you are
today!

Jump into action. One thing accomplished today moves you closer to your dreams tomorrow.

When you move toward your demand, your demand moves toward you because the Law of Attraction is at work. With every action, and every moment you follow the Demand Principle process, you close the gap.

Get on with the work now. Don't let another day go by without taking some sort of step toward the manifestation of your dream. You are the one who created it, and you are the one who must bring it to the world. Discipline yourself to keep your demands front and center, right there in front of your eyes.

To help me keep moving toward the fulfillment of my demands, I have created a Daily Discipline chart. Each morning, I set about looking at the tasks I intend to accomplish, and I don't go to bed until I have done as much as I can in the completion of them. This support tool helps me to stay true to the dream. It keeps me accountable to me. You can do it too!

Now is the time to put everything into action. If you want to bring forth your dreams and demands, you must get to "work".

No Fear

One of the things that will surely stop you in your tracks is fear.

Fear is NOT real — it's simply your "old self" crying out in an attempt to trick you back into your old ways of doing things.

As my mentor and friend Bob Proctor reminds us, *"Your paradigms are going to put up a royal battle."* It is your old paradigms (beliefs) that are trying to hold you back… and they put up a "royal battle" because they have lived inside your body and your sub-conscious mind for so long. You're kicking them out, yet they don't want to leave!

This is where most people quit, retreating to their old ways of being. Fear is a natural part of the process of change, and the current "you" isn't going to become the "you" of the future until change occurs. For you to become the best version of you, you're going to have to feel the fear but go for it anyway.

Separate yourself from the fear you feel. When you're able to observe it, you realize the fear is not you;

it is not who you are;
it doesn't even exist...
it is simply an idea inside of you
that you can choose to give power to or NOT.

"But, Peggy, how do I deal with the fear when it shows up?" you ask. Here's how you deal with it...

Divert your attention, and focus **only** on the outcome(s) you desire. Period. Connect to your demands as if they are already here and genuinely feel the gratitude for these accomplishments. Notice the fear, smile at it, and then emotionally connect with your demands.

When I wrote my first book, *On Being: The Creator of Your Destiny*, I assumed that once I had finished writing my book, the buyers would come. My initial order of 3,000 books sat in boxes inside my home; in my living room, family room, kitchen and hallway. And, then I got the idea to get my book into the bookstores. *"My books will fly off the shelves,"* I told myself.

Soon, I discovered that was not entirely accurate. Bookstores are merely consignment shops, and if your books don't sell, then they send them back to you. I was feeling fearful, because I had no job, no source of income, and, as a single mom, I was responsible for the expenses in my household.

My fearful thoughts went into overdrive, doing their best to terrify me and repeating all sorts of terrible untruths that they'd been telling me ever since I was a child. Fortunately, I was quick to recognize what was happening inside of my mind. I was engaged in a battle – "the old Peggy" versus "the new Peggy" —and I had to decide if I was going to fight fear and let faith win, or succumb to the fear. I reminded myself of an important message from a poem I read many years previously called *The Eagle Or The Wolf.*

The Eagle or The Wolf

There is a great battle that rages inside me.

One side is the soaring eagle.

Everything the eagle stands for is
good and true and beautiful, and it soars
above the clouds.

Even though it dips down into the valleys,
it lays its eggs on the mountaintops.

The other side of me is the howling wolf.

And that raging, howling wolf represents
the worst that's in me.

He eats upon my downfalls and justifies himself
by his presence in the pack.

Who wins this great battle? The one I feed.

Who do you want to be?

All at once, I knew exactly what I needed to do. So I jumped into action. I went to work learning everything I could about effective book marketing. It was the early days of the Internet, and I knew instinctively that an opportunity existed to reach a much wider audience of readers and book buyers than existed inside physical book stores. Soon, I had sold all my books online, and, in the process, I had discovered a new way of marketing that still serves me in my business today.

The good news is that I won the battle against fear – and now I get to help you do the same.

A client who has turned into a dear friend recently called me. She exclaimed, *"I just signed a contract to buy a house and I don't have the money, and I am feeling lots of fear."*

I recognized what she was talking about and knew exactly what she was going through. I said, *"You understand what is happening here, right?"*

She mumbled something that vaguely sounded like, *"Wumple gumple."*

I responded by saying, *"You are experiencing fear, and fear is not real. F.E.A.R. is an acronym for: False Evidence Appearing Real. In truth, what is happening is that you're stretching yourself. This is called growth. In order to grow into a greater, grander version of you, you may experience fear—it's often a part of the growth process."*

She listened, turned her fear into faith and purchased the home.

Anytime we step into unfamiliar territory, we will experience discomfort. Different people react differently to that discomfort depending on the number of times they have been out of their comfort zone. Therefore, each person has a different level of fear tolerance based on their exposure to it. My tolerance of fear today is certainly different than it was 20 years ago, and it may be different from yours. Yours will be different 20 years from now, too (if you follow these steps).

The best way to deal with discomfort is as an observer. Step outside the situation and look at it from afar. Of course, this will take practice. You walk after you learn how to crawl.

Taking action may cause you to feel new sensations. Those sensations are neither good nor bad, they just are. Don't let fear or discomfort or an unfamiliar feeling prevent you from pursuing your dreams. **Stand up to the fear, and watch it disappear.** When you connect to your outcome as if it is already done, the fear will go away... but you must do the work. It's not going to leave on its own.

"Sow a thought and you reap an action;
sow an act and you reap a habit;
sow a habit and you reap a character;
sow a character and you reap a destiny."

- *Ralph Waldo Emerson*

Exercise:

The Sensational Six

At the end of every day, make a list of the six tasks you WILL take the next day to advance you in the direction of your demands.

Order your list from highest priority (#1) to lowest priority (#6).

The next day, focus all of your energy and attention on the most important task until you have completed it, then put a check mark beside it, and start on the next task.

Don't move on to the next task until the preceding one has been accomplished (unless you're waiting for something or someone to complete part of it).

Repeat this every day and you will marvel at the results you get.

Chapter Fourteen
Hold The Vision

How long will it take for a poppyseed to flower or an acorn to grow into a mighty oak tree? Botanists know, for they have studied plants for centuries and have passed down their observations from generation to generation.

Were you to ask me, "*How long does it take for a demand to manifest?*" I would have to answer that it is totally dependent on many factors; some of which you have control over, and others you don't. The Law of Gestation states that *every seed must follow a process of growth, from conception to incubation through maturity to death.*

A desire is an idea that grew out of a thought, and thoughts are merely seeds of the mind for which not even the fortune teller can predict the length of time it will take to grow to maturity. Nobody can truly know.

But, as described in a previous chapter: Like rain waters and minerals nourish a seed planted in the soil, your attention and emotions feed the seed of your demand. It will take an unknown amount of time for a demand to come to pass—like everything in nature, it must follow a process.

Your responsibility as the creator of the demand is to decide on what you want, hold the vision of it materializing in your life, feel the feelings of the demand already being accomplished, and take action toward its attainment.

When a demand takes an extended period of time to materialize, many people become disheartened by a lack of external evidence that it is coming to pass. Don't rely on evidence from outside your mind as proof that you will one day have your demand! Proof in the physical that your dream has come true is the result you will manifest when you follow the Demand Principle. Holding out for validation is a losing proposition. Instead, return to the screen of your mind through visualization where you will see and feel how good it feels to have your demand. As the brilliant philosopher James Allen eloquently said: "*Wait as the one who understands.*"

Have patience and trust in the process.

When I made the decision that I would put my book, *Your Destiny Switch,* on the New York Times Best-Seller list, I spent many hours visualizing. One of the greatest things I did was find a shiny gold New York Times Best-Seller sticker, and I glued it on the front cover of my book; and then I made color copies.

By placing these mocked-up book covers all over my house and my office, it provided me with a wonderful visual and allowed me to connect to the feeling of my demand's fulfillment. I was holding tight to that dream and I wasn't letting it go.

Sometimes when I glanced at the book cover with the New York Times Best-Seller sticker on it, I would feel instant gratitude for this accomplishment. This went on for weeks! In my visualizations, I was elated because I was a New York Times Best-Selling author and every time I walked past one of many books with the shiny gold New York Times Best-Seller sticker, I stopped and connected, once again, to the gratitude. I also worked quite hard on the marketing of the book.

The day my literary agent called me to say that my book had actually made it on the New York Times Best-Seller list, I was jumping up and down like I was on a pogo stick. However, when I hung up the phone, I was filled with the strangest feeling: The fact of the matter was that in reality I didn't feel any different than I had before.

The reason why I didn't feel any different is because I had already anchored in the feeling of being a New York Times Best-Selling Author long before the book showed up on the list that the rest of the world sees. I had already been living as if it was natural for me to be a New York Times Best-Selling Author.

Do you know what I learned from that experience? I learned that you want to get to a point where it feels natural for your dream to be a reality. You must feel as if it is already done. You must feel a great sense of certainty.

How do you get there? By doing exactly as I have prescribed all throughout this book. It is no more complicated than that. It will take time, but it works for every person who follows these guidelines.

It is simple, but not easy.

The reason why it may not be easy for many people is because they don't condition themselves to follow the process. Committing to doing each of the activities in this book and following through with the work will guarantee you a successful outcome.

Create the image in your mind that will invoke the feeling that is a vibrational match with what you want to experience as if you are already doing or having it. That's what I want you to focus on like a laser.

Recreate for yourself the demands that you set for yourself, something you'd love to see for yourself; and do it with vivid, emotion-provoking, mouth-watering, goosebump-inducing detail.

Feeling Inducements

Here are some ideas to help you hold the vision and evoke the feelings of the fact that your demand is already accomplished:

- **A vacation** - Collect pictures of destinations where you'd like to visit on your next vacation to create the image that you are already in there. Photoshop yourself into the picture with your toes in the sand, or out for dinner at a wonderful restaurant with friends or sitting with your romantic partner in your first-class seats on the plane ride to your dream vacation destination. Watch videos online of the destinations and see yourself in the setting. See yourself and feel as if you are already there. What do you hear? What are you seeing? What are you feeling?
- **Finances** - Make a copy of your bank statement and replace the current balance with the balance you desire. Create a letter from the taxation office showing taxes paid in full as a visual emotion inducer. Alter the amount you owe on a credit card bill to have a zero balance, yet with the amount of credit available that you desire, for your own conditioning. Change a letter from your mortgage lender to reflect a zero balance to see the outcome you desire.
- **New car** - Have a photo taken of you in your new car. Go test drive your new car. Photoshop a picture of you handing a check to the salesman at the car dealership, paying for your new car in full. Imagine you are driving this car down the road. See yourself

driving the car along the highway. See the vehicle in your driveway or parking spot.

One of my friends sent me a framed copy of *Time Magazine* with my picture on the cover with the caption *"Person of the Year"*. When I first opened the envelope, I felt tingles all over my body. My breath caught in my throat when I first read the caption and felt the reality of those words — *"Person of the Year."* Seeing it created such a profound feeling of success that I hung it on my office wall, and I look at it as often as I can as a reminder to myself of that sensational feeling.

Let me be clear — I wasn't really on the cover of *Time Magazine*, that's not the point — the point is the feeling it evokes in me when I look at it. When I am visualizing my demands, it is that sort of feeling I want to connect to the picture to anchor it in. It is an exercise in feeling inducement. If I were to demand myself to be on the cover of *Time Magazine*, I know I would manifest this into form… just like I have with every other demand I've created.

Exercise:

Daily Discipline Chart

Create your Daily Discipline chart by replicating the one on the following pages.

This chart is one that I created for myself to ensure that I stay committed to these new disciplines.

Check off each time you implement one of these disciplines. Keep this in front of you so that you ensure you are following through and developing the disciplines for success.

"The giant trees of California were once puny saplings. The slow lapse of time has drawn nature into their mighty hearts. Just as surely as the absorption of natural forces built the giant redwoods, just as surely can you draw upon nature for GIANT POWERS."

- *Frank Channing Haddock*

Daily Discipline Chart

Activity	Monday	Tuesday	Wednesday
Listen to my Power Life Script®			
Read my Affirmations			
Write in my Gratitude Journal			
Review my List of Demands			
Demand Card			
Demand Plaque			
Mirror Work			
Six Tasks			

For the latest downloadable version, please visit:

-

Thursday	Friday	Saturday	Sunday

Chapter Fifteen

Your Success Is Guaranteed

Give yourself a big hand, for you have awakened a sleeping genie, an omnipotent force, who wants nothing more than to grant you the demands you desire; for it has only ever needed a directive from you.

Direct it using your imagination — feel your demand in its completed form as vividly real… and as surely as day turns to night, your vision will be hardened into fact before your very eyes.

When you're drifting off into sleep tonight, ask yourself again, *"Now that my dream is fulfilled, how do I feel?"*

Commit to doing this tonight. Ignite your curiosity and examine the picture you've created. Approach it like your life depended on it, because it does. See even more details than you did before.

Here are some ideas to spark your curiosity:

- *"What feelings am I now having now that my demand has been fulfilled?"*
- *"Who am I celebrating my success with?"*
- *"How are we celebrating?"*
- *"What are we saying to each other?"*
- *"Am I shouting excitedly with joy?"*
- *"What rich smells am I smelling?"*
- *"What clothes am I wearing?"*
- *"How proud of myself do I feel?"*
- *"What do I hear others saying?"*
- *"Am I jumping up and down?"*
- *"How do I feel now that my dreams are fulfilled?"*

Your new discoveries should ignite a fire inside of you that fuels your burning desire. Connect to what the fulfillment of your demands feels like. Feel elated! Ecstatic! Incredible! Unstoppable!

How will you know if you've truly connected with "that" feeling? You should feel it as if it is natural – already done – and you will have a huge smile plastered across your face with butterflies of excitement dancing in your stomach — sometimes you may even have tingles. The feeling of naturalness is the desired state you are seeking.

Go for A Perfect Match Position

As you're visualizing, you will know you have reached a *"Perfect Match Position"* when you really feel connected to your demand and you know for certain it is anchoring in, not as a possibility, but as a fact. It is already done.

There will be a point where you "know"… it is almost like you hear, *"Ding ding ding ding ding ding!"* At that point, you've arrived at a *"Perfect Match Position"*. You are totally there, completely immersed in the moment of knowing. You will feel so relaxed because your vision feels so real, so natural, so inevitable. You relax in the knowing that it is already done.

Bedtime Is The Best Time

Bedtime is the best time for you to do this kind of mental exercise… truly, it is the absolutely best time. Studies have determined that ***whatever you're thinking about in those pre-sleep moments show up in your life.*** By visualizing before you fall asleep, you're turning the work over to the sub-conscious mind to go to work on your behalf as you sleep. Invisible forces are conspiring in your favor in the background to bring it about. Whether you believe this to be true, or it sounds like baloney does not matter: So you would be best advised to harness this, believe in it, and act on it.

Then upon waking every morning, go through the same mental exercise you went through as you drifted off to sleep the night before. Stay in that same vibration, and really revel in it. Accept the fact that your demand is here now. It is, in fact, manifesting as we speak ... but your responsibility is to feel as if it is already here now.

Since everything was once a thought and you're thinking about your demand, it means your demand has actually already manifested. I call this *"The frequency of the wish fulfilled."*

Then, Do Your Work!

Success in life comes by successfully executing each day, one day at a time. Because you have completed all the exercises in the Demand Principle, you have made a plan for yourself -- for your life.

Like an architect who draws up the blueprints for his building, you need only to hammer the next nail, lay the next brick, place the next pane of glass... and slowly (or perhaps even quickly) over time, you will have constructed a beautiful life because you saw the outcome in advance and were persistent with your demand.

Your job is now to execute the plan you have created and stick to completing your Daily Disciplines today. Then do it again tomorrow. And the next day. And the day after that. The attainment of your demand is merely the stringing together of perfectly executed days, all in a row. To bring your demand to reality faster, you must execute more days in a row, making each day count.

If you lose focus or a life event knocks you off course, don't fret. Brush it off and pick back up where you left off. Beating yourself up won't help. Instead, reconnect with your demands, keeping them front and center, and then execute your Daily Disciplines one day at a time, then marvel at the manifestation.

Spend time looking at the demands you wrote in your Garden of Desires. Tick them off as soon as you have achieved them, updating your list often, adding new demands when they come to you. Visualize every chance you get. Repeat your affirmations to yourself hourly, daily. Read your demand card often. Listen to your Power Life Script®. And let every one of your Daily Disciplines inspire you to take action.

CONCEIVE. BELIEVE. ACHIEVE.

Desire-Decide-Dedicate-Demand!

Exercise:

Understand these exercises are progressive. In other words, each one builds upon itself.

When you make a habit of doing each and every one of the Daily Disciplines as directed, you will soon find that you have become a master at manifesting and can easily and effortlessly manifest anything you desire in life.

Go back to the beginning of this book and reread it often and remind yourself of these valuable ideas.

Let the process inspire you. Repeat it often. Your dreams are worth all your efforts.

Dream big...

Demand it...

Enjoy it!

“Remember, no more effort
is required to aim high in life,
to demand abundance and prosperity,
than is required to accept
misery and poverty.”

- *Napoleon Hill*

About The Author

Peggy McColl

Peggy McColl is a world-renowned wealth, business and manifestation expert as well as the New York Times Best Selling Author of *Your Destiny Switch: Master Your Key Emotions And Attract the Life of Your Dreams.*

For over 25+ years at the time of this publication, using her Power Life Script® process — along with her unique intimate understanding of the Universal Laws - she has been showing people from around the globe how to:

**Manifest any result they desire
in their personal and professional lives,
from dream homes and soulmates
to perfect health and multi-million-dollar
businesses;**

Become International Best-Selling Authors;

Create valuable products;

Build their brand worldwide;

Create wealth and complete freedom;

And much more.

She has worked with – and been endorsed by – some of the most renowned experts in the personal development field including…

Bob Proctor
Neale Donald Walsch
Jim Rohn
Dr. Wayne Dyer
Mark Victor Hansen
Caroline Myss
Gregg Braden
Debbie Ford
Arielle Ford
Hay House
Marianne Williamson
Dean Graziosi
Gay Hendricks
Marie Forleo
And many others

Peggy's special, unique & intensive programs, speaking engagements, goal achievement seminars, and best-selling books have inspired & instructed "everyday" individuals, entrepreneurs, authors and organizations to reach their maximum potential and truly take massive quantum leaps.

Peggy can help you to realize your success (both mentally, spiritually, and in "the real world"), whatever your chosen field may be! Whether you want to manifest a dream life, build your business, publish your book, or make money online, Peggy has the proven track record to help you achieve your goals.

To explore the ways in which Peggy can help you demand more of yourself and live your dreams, please visit:

www.PeggyMcColl.com

Power Life Script®

The Most Powerful Technique to Manifest Your Desires With Ease

www.PowerLifeScript.com

You may also enjoy these free resources available 24/7/365, anywhere in the world:

www.ManifestationToolbox.com

www.ManifestationPodcast.com

Printed in Great Britain
by Amazon